The Little Sower of the Night

A Camphill Story-Book

Anke Weihs-Nederhoed

The Little Sower of the Night

Stories told by
Anke Weihs-Nederhoed
to the children
of the
Camphill Rudolf Steiner School,
Aberdeen

With pictures drawn by
Günther Lehr

First Edition 1994

Published by TWT Publications Ltd.,
on behalf of
The Camphill Movement.

British Library CIP Data available

ISBN 1 897839 05 7

The publication of this book has been assisted by a grant from Camphill Blair Drummond

MADE AND PRINTED IN GREAT BRITAIN
BY CAMPHILL PRESS, BOTTON VILLAGE
DANBY, WHITBY, N. YORKSHIRE YO21 2NJ

Contents

Foreword

It was always something special to listen to Anke Weihs telling a story and experiencing a hush descending over the listeners. There was neither a word too much nor one too few when at festival times she spoke to us all. Most of her stories were told in more intimate settings, but when she spoke to us in her clear ringing voice we were taken up into an imaginary landscape. Both children and staff at the Camphill Rudolf Steiner Schools felt enriched by these events.

There are many in this enlightened age who have asked why we should interest ourselves in fairy tales, wasting children's time instead of teaching them something useful. But those who have worked with severely deprived children know how they long for such stories and how they feed on their content. Every day they would ask for 'their' story. If one faithfully responds to this need one will be surprised what changes can occur within a year. Not only will they look more healthy but they will have changed greatly in their attitudes to life.

The twentieth century has been called the century of the child, yet has there been less misunderstanding and misuse of the kingdom of childhood? Are the children of today more relaxed, healthy, happy and content? Are parents better equipped to bring up their children? Every aspect of child development has been studied and described, libraries have been filled with learned works, many provisions have been developed for all types of special needs and disturbances, and much positive help has been given. But when reading the newspapers one can only sense that the tide of despairing children, young people and parents is rising. Often one finds that children are without the inner and outer security of two loving parents and that the inner wealth of imagination has been taken from them. Many reasons can be cited to explain and justify this as perfectly 'normal'. Yet those who say this show that the thinking of our adult world has become a dried up river bed with concepts that are but barren stones in it. How can our casual thinking be re-enlivened?

A child's world is totally different from that of the adult: the child will want to linger in an experience and be one with it, while the adult will immediately arrive at a conclusion and know the intricacies of its relationships. Ideas of space and time have different dimensions for the child; our adult concepts of these are uncharted territories. Children have no difficulty in entering fairy tales where they can walk in seven league boots, journey to the end of the world, or where they can encompass a hundred year's sleep in a few minutes. Those adults who take the myths and fairy tales of the past seriously will discover that all the trials and journeys are aids for the development of the Self. In the encounter with obstacles, tasks and powers of evil, the listener will experience something of his own inner landscape. Does not every child fiercely identify with the hero of a story, with his joys and sufferings, with the relief in the overcoming of evil and administration of justice?

It is our intellectually orientated education and thinking that have dried up the wellsprings in our souls. Often it happens that in our isolation and darkness we have lost sight of what could be our real goals in life, and our massive entertainment culture helps us to forget. How many youngsters who have failed become difficult, want to 'opt out' or have lost courage, feel empty and faint-hearted! Others become destructive and violent.

Today it needs courage to tell stories again to young and old. To do so is to bring living water into our lives, to strengthen our souls with Christian and moral values, and to develop an affirmation of the worth of one's Self.

May this little book be a dedication to those who look for this living water! Just as Anke Weihs found solace, strength and renewed dignity through reading myths, tales and legends in her youth—see *Whither From Aulis: A Childhood Autobiography* by Anke Weihs (Floris Books, Edinburgh 1989)—may it also encourage those who have a gift for language and an insight into the landscape of the soul to write their own true stories!

Georg Schad
Camphill Blair Drummond

Author's Notes

Most of these stories were told in religion lessons by myself.

The Light Bearer was told at an Advent Garden celebration in Murtle.

A Child's Christmas—A kind of Fairy Tale was written for 'The Cresset'.

The Stone of Patience—inspired by a fragment of an old Greek Fairy Tale—was written for miming on Easter Saturday in Camphill.

A Spring Tale—inspired by the Class 8 lesson.

On a Green Clearing—inspired by my first sight of Fountains Abbey in Yorkshire at 4.30 one morning.

The Haven—inspired by Camphill itself.

The Green of the Valley—inspired by my first sight of Grünewald's Madonna in the Swabian Alps.

The Christmas Rose—inspired by a visit to Bruges where the Order of the Golden Fleece was founded by Philip the Good in 1429.

A Fairy Tale—in appreciation of a lecture *How can the Distress of the Soul of the Present Day be Overcome?* given by Rudolf Steiner on 10th October 1916 in Zürich.

All the others just 'came'.

Michaelmas

THE LITTLE SOWER OF THE NIGHT

When the Master of the Skies reaches the west in the evening, the great bolts of the gates of heaven are loosed with a sound like the clang of a brazen bell and the gates are flung open to receive the Master. As a sign that the sun has returned home, fiery banners are unfurled from the tops of the turrets and ripple in the wind.

The brazen sound of the opening gates wakes the Little Sower who lies asleep within. He rises and takes up his bag of seed which has served him as a pillow; he thrusts his silver sickle into his girdle and hastens through the passages of the castle which are rosy from the afterglow of the Master's return. The west wind plays upon the fiery banners like a bow upon a fine instrument.

The Lord of the Castle is host to the Sun; he has received his high guest and has conducted Him to the place within, and he now walks along the darkening ramparts of the west to see that all is well. The Little Sower of the Skies? Can it be that he is late? No. He is never late. Although time is never the same at the Castle of the Gates, the Little Sower times his rising by the entry of the sun which is the very stroke of time.

The Little Sower takes leave of the Lord of the Castle to begin his night's labour and goes out by a small low gate at the side, taking his little plough with him.

Out on the fields of the night, the Little Sower ploughs the furrows of the sky. They are not straight furrows like ours down here on earth. The furrows of the fields of the sky circle and loop and loop again and are of great depth and breadth and length. The Little Sower labours swiftly and silently—by the time the fiery banners have been lowered from the turrets in the west, his furrows are ready. He opens his bag and sows his seed which straightway springs up and flowers in countless silver blossoms on the fields of the night, petals trembling like the iridescent wings of hovering butterflies. The Little Sower laughs with joy to see the crop and flings his sickle high up in the sky where it hangs, waiting for the harvest.

Up there among the silver flowers of the night, there is a fragrance that we cannot sense down here on earth—perhaps only when we smell a rose. Like the diligent bees down here in our gardens which gather the pollen from the blossoms for their honey, up there the souls of those who have died to the earth gather the pollen from the silver flowers of the stars and spread the unearthly fragrance from one end of the universe to the other.

Silently, swiftly the Little Sower walks the marches of the night—and when the midnight hour strikes in the heights he reaches for his sickle and begins the harvest.

Swish, swish goes the delicate blade of the silver sickle over the fields of the night. Straightway the Little Sower gathers up the seed into his bag. Sometimes a seed is lost. Look! Did you not see it flashing down from the heights almost to your very feet? We call it a shooting star.

The Little Sower has but a given time for his labours, but he always finishes the moment the Gates of the East are loosed with a song that of all the creatures down here on earth, only the birds know and sing in jubilation. On the rising swell of the morning song, the Master of the Skies goes out upon his journey across the vault above and treads the infinite blue of the fields of the skies with measured step. Under his tread, the pollen shed from the silver blossoms of the night rises and billows upwards. Do you see it? The clouds! And when the pollen is rich and heavy, the clouds loose rain upon the earth and each droplet carries some of the sparkling sweetness of the skies downwards and quenches the thirst of the earth. Look! You can see a diamond droplet resting in the heart of the flowers among the grasses in the fields in the early morning.

Day has begun. The Little Sower is spent. Through a small low gate at the side, he slips into the Castle, bearing his heavy bag of seed. He must account for his work to the Lord of the Castle before he goes to rest. The Lord of the Castle weighs the seed on his balances and pronounces it good.

Blinded by the daylight, the Little Sower goes to his rest. He lays his head upon the bag of seed which serves him as a pillow and slumbers—until in the evening he is wakened by the brazen clang of the Gates of the West that open to receive the sun, and he rises to begin his labours on the deep wide fields of the night.

Whose servant is the Little Sower? He is the servant of the Lord of the Castle.

Who is the Lord of the Castle? He is the Archangel Michael who is host to the Master of the Skies.

Who is the Master of the Skies? The Master of the Skies is Christ Who walks in the sun.

Tell me one thing more: what is that place within, to which the Master returns? The place within is a tiny chamber, dark and tight and throbbing with longing that in time the harvest of the fields down here on earth be as good and as sparkling as the harvest up there in the night sky. It is to that narrow throbbing chamber that the Master returns each night when He has traversed the heavens. Michael, his host, knows the place where the Master chooses to dwell and he knows the longing that fills it. Therefore he stands there to open the gates each night.

SOMETHING FOR NOTHING

Long ago in the dim past, three men plodded along the dusty road that leads all men away from Paradise into the grey, grey world. It was an autumn evening and along the sides of the road there stretched great fields that had been harvested. The stubble shone bluntly in the slanting evening sunlight. The three wanderers stopped and, looking over the fields, they began to bemoan the injustice that favours a few and deprives the many of the good things of the earth. Why must a man work so hard to feed himself? Why cannot something, just a little something, be given a man without having to toil and labour from morning till night? Why must we be eternally blamed for Adam's misuse of the gifts of God? What an injustice it is to blame us all for the sins of the one! The world will come to a sorry end if God Himself is so unjust. We cry defiance in the face of heaven: give us our due, we have a right to it!

As the three men stood by the field filling the still autumn air with their ranting, a labourer drew near and spoke to them: "Have done with your noise and listen to me. I shall give you something for nothing. You shall reap what you have not sown. Look to the far end of this field—do you see the two sacks there?" The three men turned to peer across the lengthening shadows. "One is a sack of corn," said the labourer, "the other a sack of gold received in payment for other corn I have harvested. My barns and my money chests are full. These two sacks are left over and you may have them. It is a pity that they are only two while you are three, but you must solve that among yourselves." With these words, the labourer left them and went along the road the way they had come.

The three men (they were called Thomas, Richard and Harold) began to argue about the two sacks, each one feeling that he was worthier to have the sack of gold than his companions—until it began to get dark.

"We shall no longer be able to see where the sacks are," said Harold, "let us quickly decide what to do."

"I have it," cried Richard, "let the three of us run a race—the one who wins gets the gold, the second gets the corn, and the third will have to be the loser."

"What a good way to solve the question," said Thomas and Harold, and all three lined up by the fence, one foot forward and eyes on the two sacks at the far end of the field.

"Go!" they shouted and off they raced across the stubble. Thomas was the nimblest and reached the sacks first and soon after, Richard came panting along; far behind came poor Harry stumbling over the hidden furrows.

"Well," said Tom, "it is clear that I am the winner and that the sack of gold is mine. And you, Dick, are not so badly off—you can sell your sack of corn for a good amount of money. Only poor old Harry, you were always the slowest. Never mind; you can help us to carry our sacks when they get too heavy and we shall pay you something for that!"

Poor Harry thought to himself: "That is the end of getting something for nothing for me."

Now the night had deepened and the forms and colours of the earth had merged into the darkness that hides all things. Tom shouldered his heavy sack of gold, Dick his sack of corn, and Harry followed behind them with nothing to carry.

They soon found their way back to the long, long road again and each went on silently, thinking his own thoughts. At last the road began to rise and wind its way up over the crest of a hill between two mountains.

Tom began to strain under his load and could hardly place one foot before the other. "Brother," he gasped to Harry, "take my sack for a while and carry it for me across yonder pass. Wait for me when you come down on the other side, for I must stay here and rest." Harry willingly took up the sack of gold and he and Dick went on up the winding road over the top of the hill and down on the other side.

Now in the east, the darkness was beginning to grow thin like a veil that is stretched until it dissolves and soon the light of a new day spread over the earth and its creatures. Only Dick and Harry were very weary for they had walked and climbed throughout the night.

"Let us lie down here on the grass and sleep," said Dick, "until Tom catches up with us." They put their sacks down, laid their heads upon them and slept.

When they awoke, it was midday by the look of the sun, but no Tom was to be seen.

"Something must have happened to him," said Dick, "I shall go back and look for him. You, Harry, wait here until we both return."

"Very well," said Harry, and watched Dick climb the hill until he disappeared over the top.

The day was hot and the hours followed slowly upon one another. Harry felt the pangs of hunger and thirst. "There will be no harm in my looking for something to eat and drink," he thought. He covered the sacks with branches so that a chance wanderer would not see them and went into the woods where he found nuts and late berries and a clear spring of water.

When the sun began to lose its height, Harry went back to the two sacks which were still where he had left them, but there was no sign of either Dick or Tom nor could he see their forms coming up over the hilltop.

It grew dark and still Harry waited for his two companions. He waited all night and they did not come. "What shall I do?" he thought. "Shall I leave the sacks and go back and look for them, or what if harm

should come to the sacks while I am away? Yet I cannot take both of them on my back and climb that hill again." With these thoughts the day waxed, but still Tom and Dick did not appear.

When the sun had reached the height of noon, Harry again went in search of food. This time he went further and it was not long before he heard the sound of rushing water, and going still further, he saw a mighty river in the distance. Fetching the two sacks, with great effort, he reached the banks of the river on the other shore of which he saw the gleaming towers of a city. He had never been in a city before and the longing to see one close at hand was sharp, and in that moment, he saw a boat tied to a stump at his feet. He heaved both sacks into the boat, rejoicing in his good fortune, and untied the rope that held the boat fast. In so doing, he missed his footing and slipped on the mud, losing his grip on the rope. The swift current of the river took possession of the boat and its burden and down the river it went, swirling and turning whithersoever the current took it until it was out of poor Harry's sight.

We must now leave Harry sitting forlorn on the banks of the river. Who knows? Maybe he found Tom and Dick again and if so, they would all three be exactly where they were at the beginning of our story—having nothing for nothing.

The labourer's gifts were now alone in the world—the sack of corn and the sack of gold. They took their toll of peace between men and indeed of their lives, too. They were the worst of wanderers, these two. From city to city, from town to town, from house to house they went, never settling and becoming the rightful heritage of any, and whatsoever man or ruler or state gained possession of them for a time had to suffer their loss again and the loss of much more besides.

Nation fought nation; whole peoples fought in the struggle to possess the corn and the gold, and in one of these great battles, the two sacks were captured by a tyrant from the east (or was it from the west?), and were carried out to sea in ships. At sea those ships ran into a storm of great violence and were wrecked, and the tyrant and his men and his goods went to the bottom of the ocean.

And now the labourer thought to recall the gifts he had given to men for nothing and did so in this wise.

Far out at sea in the west of the world, there lay a little rocky windswept island. Its only inhabitant besides the birds was a monk who had been the sole survivor of his ship which was wrecked on the rocks. In gratitude to the Holy Spirit, he built a little chapel out of the stones and mud of the island and with much diligence shaped a cross of stone for the little stone altar. Since the day of his arrival on the island, it was his custom to walk each morning along the shore where the salt waves curled over the white sands and to pick up anything that was washed ashore, whether a gull's feather or fragment of weed, whether flotsam or jetsam, and take it to the little chapel to offer it up, invoking the blessing of Christ on its origin.

One radiant morning long after the beginning of our story, the monk walked around his island as was his wont, his heart atune to the music of the water gurgling in and out of the crevices in the rocks. The waves swelled and dipped and tossed the light bodies of the gulls upon their foamy crests. The monk paused to watch them and from them his gaze wandered further out to sea, piercing in its intensity beyond the great curved line of the horizon. All at once between the infinite and the little island upon which he stood, he perceived a dark object on the surface of the sea. His heart leapt with the sudden hope that it might be a boat, for he had neither seen nor spoken to another fellow human being since the day he was shipwrecked, and his soul was thirsty for human exchange. But because the wind and the waves were driving the dark object swiftly towards his island, he soon saw that it was not a boat and that it was merely a broken plank upon which lay two sodden sacks. The shore waves soon took the plank into their play and washed it up onto the sands together with the sacks. The monk ran forward thinking: "What a beautiful offering has come my way this day! That plank will make a table-top for my altar. I shall take it up to my chapel and shall fetch the sacks, whatever they may contain, later."

He raised the broad plank upon his head and carried it to the chapel where he offered it up to his Lord Christ to be a table-top for the altar, and when he laid it on the stone, it neither shook nor swerved nor moved again.

After this, the monk returned to the beach where the departing tide had left the two sacks drying in the sun. He did not examine their content, but trusting that his Lord would accept them, he set to work to haul them to the chapel, first the one a little way, then the other, and again the first by stages, until, using all his strength, he reached the chapel with both sacks. Once inside, he pulled them over the stone floor and heaved first the one and then the other onto the altar. Then he prayed: "My Lord, never has any offering of mine been so heavy as this that I bring today. I do not know what I have brought You from the sea and perhaps the very heaviness of it is of the nature of misery and discord; nevertheless, I pray that the all-transforming power of Your light, O Christ my Master, will change this burden into what was intended with it at its origin."

Thus the monk prayed and when he perceived the light of Christ with his inner eye, he opened his bodily eyes and saw that the two sacks had become part of Christ—were His Body and His Blood, the bread and the wine He gave to heal the wounds men inflicted on themselves.

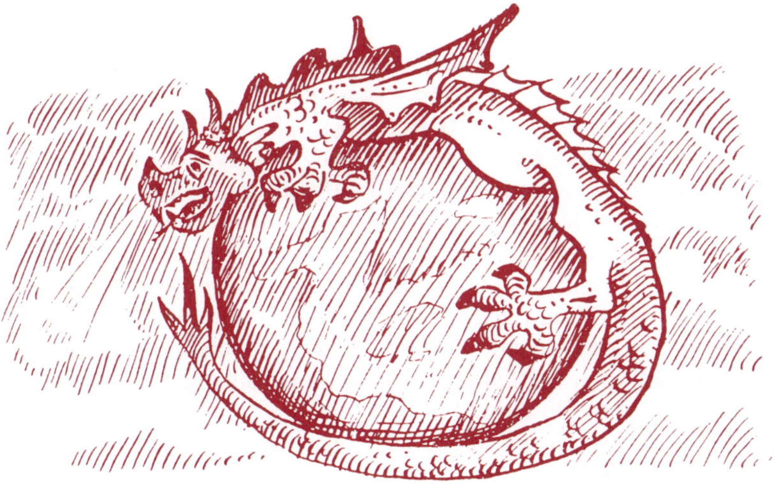

THE EIGHTH SON

There was once a king who had seven sons. There was an eighth besides but he was too young to be of much account. They lived in a palace high up above windswept heights. The queen, their mother, had died in bringing forth the eighth; her cloak waved as the banner from the tip of the highest tower—during day a bridal veil, during night a bejeweled scroll.

The seven princes grew into manhood. They were noble and brave in all respects and their deeds were determined and straightforward and cast no shadows. Only the youngest, the eighth, seemed to be made of other stuff. He was neither good nor evil nor brave as his brothers were. His words were often twisted so that no one could grasp their meaning and his deeds recondite and some thought thievish and envious. Nonetheless, one thing about him was clear and straight—his playing of the lyre. This had nothing of seductiveness or desire or sultry fire. His melodies came from the light-filled regions touched by the tips of his mother's cloak as it fluttered high above the palace and were rivulets of pure tone trickling down from the silvery heights of spirit, incomprehensible to his father and brothers, yet filling the great hall of the palace with rare peace when he played. Otherwise, the eighth son was strange and untransparent, but he had little bearing on his father's court for all his strangeness.

The time came when the old king saw that his palace was too small to contain his seven sons who were now ready to take on the kingdoms predestined for them. He sent for his sons and went into the great hall to await their coming. The hall was high and long, its vaulted ceiling was indigo like the sky at midnight. The pillars were the colour of ivory and the arches were rilled with ruby fillets. The walls were deep sea-green, the floor of opalescent colours, ever-moving like the surface of the sea. Through the fluted windows came soft rosy light, filling the hall with a living glow.

The old king sat on his ancient throne and into the hall came his seven sons, their steps ringing and the arches taking up the echo. The eighth one came too, but no one noticed him standing in the shadows beneath the pillars.

The old king opened his mind to his seven sons. The things they heard him speak of were profound and mysterious and each felt the sanctity of the moment. "Come with me, my sons, to the tower. From there shall you enter the seven realms that are your predestined kingdoms."

He rose from his throne and led the way out of the hall through long passages, up winding steps, dim at first, then becoming ever brighter, to the top of the highest tower. The view from there was awe-inspiring and no words can describe it for it reached into the infinite above, below and round about. The seven princes stood in silence with their old father, each listening to the fluttering of their mother's cloak waving close above them.

Then the moment of holy silence broke. The old king raised his hand in command and the seven realms circled in majesty and fiery glow, nearer and nearer the tower, dipping in reverence as they passed the banner. "The time is ripe," cried the old king, "Your kingdoms have come to your feet!"

As each fiery sphere, circling in serene rhythms, dipped down to the tower, one of the seven princes entered its glowing orb, the old king sealing each departure with ancient gestures of ordination.

When all the seven sons had gone from the tower, the gleaming circle of the seven orbs swung back into its shining course and new epochs began.

Alone in the tower, the old king turned to descend. There in the shadows stood his eighth son. He looked infinitely downcast as he stood before his father.

"Sire, have you nothing for me? I too am your son," he said softly.

"Your mother bore your brothers according to ancient prophecies; harmony and the jubilation of the heavens surrounded their births. Your own foretelling was obscure, you were born out of harmony, your birth took your mother's life, and I, your father, have nothing to give you."

The old king's words were hard. Unutterable sorrow, clear and open, shone in the eyes of the eighth son. The old king's heart was stirred.

"Stay with me, my little son. I am alone now in these lofty halls. You can play to me on your lyre; incomprehensible though your melodies may be, I think your mother would have cherished them."

"No, sire, let me go too; my melodies will die if I stay."

The old king led his remaining son to the crystal window of the tower. The youth scanned the infinite spaces round about. Above in remote splendour, he saw the seven kingdoms of his brothers. Beyond there was the bright horizon of eternity; below, the mists of a hidden far distant future.

"Where will you go, my son, into the nothingness?"

For a while the youth was silent. All at once, far below he saw a tiny object swimming on the crests of a misty restless sea. His heart leapt: "Father, do you see that tiny speck far down below? Would that not be a kingdom for me? It does not matter that it is small as long as it can be my own."

The old king answered in a voice that rumbled through the passages like muffled thunder: "Do not speak of that speck, son. It is only dust cast off the radiance of the all-highest. It signifies eternal shame and will one day sink into oblivion."

The eighth son's countenance was aflame, his heart aquiver: "Father, let me go there, for you know that shame is more akin to me than the splendour of your palace. You yourself have said my birth was obscure."

"You do not know what you are saying," the old king spoke, clouds of anger gathering on his brow. "I told you it was a speck of dust, for so it seems from these heights. Nevertheless, that speck has life and if you would look at it more closely, you would see an evil monster swimming in nameless and bitter waters, a threat to the radiance of the universe, a blot on the cosmos. I command you not to speak of this thing again."

The flames died down in the countenance of the eighth son; he became pale and his heart like cool metal. He said nothing further to his father of this matter, but turned and followed him out of the tower, the whispering of his mother's mantle in the wind growing fainter as they descended.

That evening when the rosy glow in the hall deepened into red, when the stars on the ceiling cast silver rays into the shifting colours of the palace floor, the young prince sat at his father's feet and played his lyre. The old king bowed his head and listened to the sweet serenity of the tones. The circling of the seven glowing kingdoms above sent beams of many-coloured light in measured intervals into the hall. The music pervaded the living shadows with its own pure essence. The peace of a divine order reigned.

After a time, the youth laid aside his lyre. A hush fell over the palace; soft blue shadows crept beneath the arches of the pillars. The old king felt blissful weariness and rose and went to his rest.

The shadows gathered closer around the eighth son and enveloped him like a cloak. With his lyre slung over his shoulder and the cloak of shadows wrapped around him, he left his father's palace.

His path lay downwards through darkness and dense mists. He would often have lost his way had he not been pulled down steadily by an unknown, unrelenting force. At last his feet touched upon chill grey waters and ahead of him, looming up in the fog, the dread monster of which his father had spoken lay upon the waters. Boundless fear seized the youth and the longing for his mother coursed through his veins as he faced the monster, sensing its evil life, smelling the dank fumes around it, hearing the harsh sounds from within its hideous body.

"What have I done?" he cried in anguish. The monster hearing the cry over the leaden waters was roused and turned its gloating visage towards the youth, the while moving nearer, looming ever more terrible as it came.

Fear almost extinguished the life in the youth. On the brink of annihilation, for want of any other help, he took his lyre into his hands and played a melody he had never played before. There was no one there to hear it save the monster. From the youth to the monster went the unwitnessed communion in grey and watery wastes.

The silvery power of the music was potent; it softened the huge body of the monster and its restlessness was anchored in the hold of the bed of the ocean. Its evil life became the growing and decaying of the plants and other life upon the island, its dank breath the ever-changing weather, the driving of the wind, the soft play of light in the clouds, the sweet breath of spring. Its harsh sounds died away into the song of the birds, the lowing of cattle, the whispering of the grasses, the lapping of the waves at the fringe of the shores, the bubbling of mountain springs.

This fair island became the kingdom of the youth. It was full of ever-changing life; all that grew and lived on it died and decayed to live anew, full of the sweetness and hope of becoming, of losing and regaining, so young, so free, so loosened from the timeless splendour of his father's ancient halls.

Corn grew and ripened, grapes swelled and their purple juice ran into golden cups. But always dangerous and precarious was the life of that little kingdom established on the back of the monster—for deep below the sweetness of the meadows, beneath the coolness of the forests, down below the glittering metal mines, there lurked the old dark power of the blood of the dragon, clotted with shame and avarice, lusting for destruction, but asleep.

Yet this dormant evil could be roused by a thoughtless word spoken by any of those who came to live on the island as subjects of the young king, or by the taint of a loveless deed that trickled through the crevices in the rocks, stirring the slumbering embers of the fires of the dragon's blood.

Ever and again it was the young king who quenched those unholy fires, whose gaze was ever alert, whose ears always strained beyond the sound of his own voice, because he knew of the nature of his island kingdom and knew, too, of the powers that transform and heal.

And so whenever danger threatened from below, he took his lyre into his hands and entered into communion with the dragon.

It was not a communion of power or of magic; it was the communion of compassion. It was a song of love he sang, a song of freedom.

Have you ever heard it sung? Come, sing it if you know it—for the eighth son has left his kingdom to us.

THEN SHALL TWO BE IN THE FIELD...

Once there were two brothers who lived on the land. From childhood on, they had tilled the soil. They lived at peace with one another, but their life was hard and the plot of earth upon which they lived, exacting. Whenever they slackened in diligence, the earth revenged itself and brought forth sparsely.

When the weather was clear, the heavens high-arched and blue, and the young corn shimmering green broke through the brown furrows, the words the brothers exchanged were cheerful and their hearts were light as the white clouds overhead or as the flight of the larks. But when grey folds of fog hung heavy over the hills in the autumn, choking the valleys, and dampness seeped into all corners or the blast of storms raged over the land, the brothers were overwhelmed by hopelessness and a greyness far emptier than the greyness that stretched over the fields towards the dark mountains in the distance crept into their hearts. Was not life senseless, the eternal cycle of the year merciless and the lot of men as dim as the death that comes at the end of all our ways? And even if the corn grows and ripens, it dies and is made into bread to nourish men in order that they too die.

Yet when the harvest was rich and the brothers earned good money, these sorry questions were forgotten for a time and they went about their work with light minds, until the sadness came again, heavy and grey, to be relieved by the soaring gladness in their hearts in the spring. So do men's souls sway, as the loose twig hanging on the bough of a tree sways in the wind.

Evil times came and reigned over the earth. There was fearful news of wars and catastrophes and of hatred and violence. The wavering souls of the brothers froze in fear as the twig freezes in the winter frost, unable to move lest it break.

When a man has joy, he cannot so easily share his joy with others. When a man has fear, the fear seems to share itself. He who first has fear need do nothing to impart it to others; fear creeps like underground cold fire from place to place to flare up treacherously and possess the weak. So the brothers worked on their fields and the fear of the oncoming evils in the world was the unvoiced driving force in all their labour.

Once, after they had done a hard day's work and returned to their little house in the evening, they were too benumbed by fear to eat. They longed only for that deep sleep that puts men's hearts to rest in unknown regions. So they lay down in their beds and submerged themselves in the deep ocean of slumber where the torturing fears of the day are silently drowned for a time, even if the waves of disaster beat ceaselessly on the bleak shores of the waking world.

The two brothers lay still. All at once the door to their room opened softly. A dim blue light casting no shadows pervaded the darkness and within its shifting iridescence went a form, a human form, that was the source of the light. The form bent over the one brother and gently called him by name: "Rise up and come with me. Let me take the fear away from you. Come!" The young man groaned as his soul rose up out of the obscure and colourless region of sleep and felt pained as it hovered on the brink of waking: "Let me sleep," he sighed, "sleep alone can help." He closed his eyes and his soul sank back into the deep well of sleep. The stranger perceived the fleeting soul and compassion glowed in his eyes, yet he made no move to summon it back. The young man turned to the wall and began to breathe heavily.

The delicate bluish rays of light flooded through the room as soundlessly the stranger moved to the bed of the other brother. Bending over him, he called softly: "Awake and follow me. Let me turn your fear into hope." The soul of the other brother heard and hurried to the surface of consciousness. It perceived the dim light and divined that it was neither the daylight nor a light of the night. It was a different light which cannot be sensed by the eyes. It is a tender light of unnameable quality and can be seen by searching hearts in rare moments. The soul of the other brother crossed the barrier of waking and said to the stranger: "I shall follow you."

The stranger led him out of the house into the quiet dark night. He walked soundlessly ahead, a pillar of delicate light, and although no blade of grass, no root, no stone reflected his light, the other brother followed behind as though his very feet were able to see.

They passed over dark pastures, brooks and hedges, past sleeping villages, through stony valleys, out again onto plains, over lakes, through forests, further and further until they reached the foot of a great mountain. Here the stranger stayed his steps and said to the other brother: "Turn around and tell me what you see." The man turned around. The sky was greying before the dawn of another day. The rough earth lay spread out before him with its sharp upcast cliffs, its rivers, deserts, seas, hills, then—cities, factories, mines, houses, churches, palaces, shacks, and traffic, hospitals, slums and over everything the smouldering dust of wars. The earth seemed to be a terrible place to the man and the fear he knew so well pounded in his veins. He endeavoured to answer his companion, but could form no words. "Now look up," said the stranger.

The man looked up to the remote peak of the mountain at the foot of which they were standing, and saw wisps of silvery mists hovering high up and a pale little star shining faintly through. The mountain peak seemed cold and forbidding and it sent the chill of a new kind of fear into the heart of the man. Doubt in his quiet companion troubled his mind and he was scarcely able to describe what he saw.

"Will you go with me?" asked the stranger, "we have a long way to go and it leads upwards." He pointed to a tiny path that wound up the side of the mountain. Burning tears shot into the eyes of the man. "Come," whispered the stranger and the other brother stumbled after him.

They climbed for a long time. Deep silence reigned round about and although it seemed to be bright above them, their path wound through shadows. Tears ran unceasingly down the cheeks of the man, welling up out of the bottomless spring of human loneliness, but the stiffness of fear was loosened in the pain of his great sadness. Blindly, knowing now that the stranger meant him no harm, he followed with unseeing eyes.

After a long time, he heard the voice of the stranger: "Dry your tears and look!" The man did as he was commanded. Far down below he beheld the infinity of space and among the manifoldness of circling spheres in the vastness, he saw the earth-body, a burning, unquiet planet, both dark and light, small yet powerful and dangerous. It seemed out of place among the other serene starry bodies, and yet augered future promise.

Above him, the peak of the mountain was nearer, spangled with glistening crystal gullies and ravines out of which shot flames of silver fire. He saw that the mountain received its radiance from the unearthly iridescence of the star above which no longer hung pale in the sky but spread a living glow over and around the summit like a mantle of light. The soul of the man was filled with awe and a wondrous sense of balance and certainty flowed through his being. He felt deep gratitude to the stranger who had led him here and turning to him, saw how the dim blue light that had woven in and out of his form now came to rest in a steady brightness as though he were at home on these sublime heights. "We have almost reached our goal," said his guide and he led the man upwards towards the gleaming summit. As they ascended, a gentle warmth flowed down from above and took the man up in unspeakable tenderness.

The silvery sparks from the crystalline gullies round the summit paled in the golden light that shone ever more powerfully from the star. The stranger led the brother swiftly to the highest point of the peak into the light of the sun and the brother perceived how the stranger's light united with the sun's light and how the sunlight became brighter in response.

Now the man recognised the high nature of his guide and jubilating within, he called out his name. The other said: "Turn again and look down to where you came from."

The man looked down—far, far down in immeasurable distance, he saw a pale little star, hovering uncertainly in the indigo infinite. As he gazed on it, he discerned its faint shadow—cross-shaped. Round about circled the other bright stars but none save the earth-star cast a shadow, none save the earth bore a cross.

"Now you see the earth in truth," spoke his high leader, "you see it from the place where the gods are ever watching it. For in that pale little star down there lie the hopes, the will, the love of the gods, their suffering and their joy. It was I Who inscribed the Cross into the shadow of the earth as the mark of Love and one day when gods and men strive knowingly together, that star will shine like no other. I have shown you what the gods behold so that your fear can be transmuted into faith and that you may be able to help others overcome fear. But now come to my table and eat before you take the long way back to earth."

The man sat down at the Master's table and received food and drink from His hands. The bread contained the toil of countless human harvests; the wine the blood of countless human wounds—all caught up and treasured and transmuted in the heights.

Now he was on his way down. Down he wound on the little path—swiftly. As he descended, the golden starlight gradually withdrew into the remote heights. The silvery wisps of mist still played around the crystalline peak of the mountain. Then denser mists enveloped the summit, hiding it, and far, far above hovered a pale little star.

Down below that other star had waxed and grown, its pallor changing into a dull red glow. At times its shadow was almost invisible, but never quite. Mightier and mightier the earth became in the sight of the man. As he drew near the foot of the mountain, its great forms and shapes loomed up. He heard the sound of the winds howling over the bleak plains, the roaring of turbulent seas, the rushing of torrents. He saw the many things, big and small, ugly and beautiful made by men; he heard the noise and clamour of their lives, and a feeling of love to the earth, to its creatures and to their needs such as he had never known before filled his breast. He descended to the plain as the bridegroom descends to greet his bride.

The early morning wind blew over the fields. The stacks of corn glistened in the autumn frost. In the east the sun was rising, casting light gently over the stubble. The other brother walked swiftly towards his little house where his brother lay in his bed, sleeping soundly. He bent over him for a moment and saw him anew; the longing to serve him, to live for him filled his heart. Then he lay down in his own bed for a while, for the hour of rising had not yet come.

Advent and Christmas

THE LIGHT BEARER

The world had become a deep valley choked with the shadows of sorrow and death. Light no longer shone in the houses of men and their minds were dark, and fire no longer burned on their hearths or in their hearts. The paths from one place to another were unlit and cold cruel winds swept over the land, leaving men's souls numb with misery as they huddled in their darkened dwellings. Evil walked in the cover of darkness and its grip lay upon everything.

High above the valley of the world on distant lofty peaks that could neither be seen nor scaled by men, there lived a king with two princes and his only son. The palace was filled with floods of rosy glow that radiated from a crystal bowl that was kept there and held eternal living light. This was the origin of all life and light and warmth and was the most holy thing in the universe. The delicate rainbow floods of iridescent fire were so radiant that none but the king and the princes and his son could behold them face to face; even the servants of the king, light though they were, had to cover their eyes in the presence of the living light.

From far down below faint cries of despair rose to the hearing of the king whose heart began to fill with compassion for the unhappy ones from whom the light had gone because of their misuse of it and their sinfulness, and he resolved to restore light to the world if one could be found to bear it downward.

The king called the princes and his son and a council took place. The eldest prince was entrusted with the mission of restoring the living light to the world below.

The eldest prince was clever and powerful. He constructed a lamp in which the living light could be safely carried and when it was finished, he filled it from the wellspring of the crystal bowl, secured it tightly and took leave of the king.

Down the dark descent he went towards the dim valley below, the lamp with its sacred fire concealed beneath his cloak. No man saw his coming and even when he began to move among the people in the valley, they barely sensed his presence until he spoke to them of the prize he held hidden and stirred in them the sharp desire to know what it was.

Here and there, he threw back his cloak and revealed the living light in his lamp and men gathered around him begging for a droplet to lighten their darkness, but the lamp was secured so tightly that he could not open it and give the light away. So he had to cover it up again and go on to other parts, leaving the valley darker and colder than it was before. Men felt cheated and rose up in hatred against one another and against the prince. Terrible deeds were done and the prince fled in fear from the world and returned to the king above, having failed in his mission. But the king's heart was straining in compassion that could no longer be quelled and he sent the second prince to the world below to restore the living light to men.

The second prince was beautiful and proud. He lost no time but fashioned a torch which he plunged into the depths of the crystal bowl, drawing it out ablaze. Holding the torch high above his head, he went down the steep descent, the night sky alight with the flames. All men saw him coming and went to meet him as he strode among the multitudes, brandishing his torch like a banner. Sparks flew up and trees caught fire and forests began to burn. At first the people laughed to see so much brightness, but as the fire swept over their fields and burned down their houses and caught many of them in its clutches, they cried out in anguish and plunged into the seas to save themselves. The world burned and the second prince fled from his handiwork in shame, leaving ashes and untold suffering in his wake, and stood before the king unable to raise his eyes.

There was silence in the palace for a long space of time.

The king's own son drew near to his father's throne: "Send me into the world, father, to take the living light to men." "My son," said the king "these two mighty princes have failed terribly and the plight of men in the world is worse than before. Neither lamp nor torch can carry the holy light. There is no way to take it back to the world."

"I will drink it and be the carrier myself," said his son. "O my beloved," said the king "the living light will consume you with pain."

"My father, it is your own compassion that sends me into the world. Let me go."

"Go then, my beloved son, and do what has to be done."

The king's son drew near to the crystal bowl of living light. Gently he cupped his hands and filled them and drank. The living light coursed through his body from his hands to his feet filling it with unspeakable pain, and he went out into the night, a tender luminescence lighting up the darkness around and before him.

A few wakeful men saw his coming in the night and took him into their houses. To all those who received him he gave of himself, and with himself he gave the living light, so sweet, so infinitely comforting, so steadfast and strong. As he went from place to place, himself ever more consumed by the pain of the living light within him, more and more lights began to burn in the houses of men, shedding brightness into the darkness outside and giving warmth to those who were cold, giving grace and comfort and healing to the sorrowful hearts of men.

And so the living light was restored to the world.

Christmas Dreams

Christmas time is a time of dreams when the nights are transparent and wisps of heavenly substance mingle with the visible things of the earth and catch on the corners of men's minds, filling them with divining.

The trees were stark and silent at the edge of the forest and the withered leaves lying around their roots did not stir. Then out of the north a wild tempest rose and swept over the earth, whipping up the withered leaves and driving them into wasted regions.

Those leaves were the prayers of children; they were once green with hope, then golden with faith and were now faded and forgotten. The tempest was sweeping them out of the world so that their sighing could no longer be heard.

But high up in the sky, the sickle boat of the moon sailed the oceans of the universe and in the boat sat a maiden fishing with a net of silver. When she looked down and saw the tempest raging over the earth, she cast her net and caught the faded and dying prayers of the children before they were swept into nothingness. The silver net became heavy with prayers and the maiden drew it up away from the evil breath of the tempest to the shores of the pools of the moon.

There she opened her net and emptied its contents into the pools of the moon and the prayers swam like rosy little fishes, streaking silver in the shimmering waters. The sickle boat sailed on with the maiden who fished with her net as before.

But then the maiden fell out of her boat onto the earth where she had to live in a house. Her silver net was gone, too, and she began to weave another one for her fishing. This net was red because it was made of blood and the maiden often wept as she tied its many knots.

When all the knots of the net of blood were tied, the maiden went in search of a place to fish. She came to a pool high up among the snow-covered peaks of the mountains, which was as blue as the eye of heaven and mirrored the remote summits round about.

The maiden found a tiny black boat tied to the edge of the pool. She loosed it and rowed onto the waters and floated over the clear images on the surface of the pool, causing them to tremble. Her red net lay across the rim of the boat, but she saw no fish. Instead she gazed down to the very bottom of the pool which was as clear as glass.

From the depths, huge whales came swimming and darkened the pool, troubling the waters and the bright images on them, and the maiden was struck with fear. More and more whales filled the pool and there was chaos in the waters so that the little boat tossed about in frenzy.

Then from above, the rosy silver fishes in the pools of the moon cast their shining reflections down onto the pool beneath and the great whales sank back into the depths. The water became calm and the lofty mountain peaks gleamed perfectly on its surface.

Among the silver fishes in the pools of the moon there was a golden fish as bright as the sun. The maiden cast her blood red net and caught the golden fish and drew it into her boat.

Dawn poured molten light down the slopes of the mountains and the blue pool was flooded with gold. The little black boat carried the maiden to the shore and she, holding the golden fish to her heart, went down to her house in the valley.

It was winter and the forest was very dark for it was almost the darkest night. Snow began to fall through the still air to lie gently on the ground and along the twigs of the trees.

Midnight came. High up beyond the mountains a bell unlike any bell on earth began to ring. The ringing was faint at first, but then the tones descended from the mountains in opalescent globes of pure sound and rolled through the forest down into the valley. As the clear round tones sounded through the forest, each snowflake lit up like a

tiny lamp as it fell softly to the earth where it lay with all the other burning snowflakes, so that the whole forest had a crystal carpet of fire. The sap in the trees awoke to the ringing of the bell and shone like golden oil in the dark trunks; rabbits hopped over the fiery snow, their long ears glowing from within, and the deer trod gently through the bright trees with their antlers aflame on their lovely heads.

Louder and clearer rang the bell, and every pine-cone, every whitened twig and every rolling snowdrift burned with transparent fire. The blue shadows beneath the long low branches of the fir trees were invaded by the rosy glow. It was a night of living light in the darkness.

Then down from the mountains through the trees came another light, a light within the light, and it came as a Child swiftly through the golden night. The opalescent globes of tone hovered in the still air around the Child as it went its way over the fiery carpet of snowflakes. The long rosy ears of the rabbits listened and the deer waited along the path and bowed their flaming antlers before the Child; the trees stood like bright crosses on the way. The whole forest was aglow with light; even the dim valley below was touched, and the mountains round about were lit up to their very peaks which gleamed against the midnight sky.

Then the Child was gone down into the valley and one by one the lights in the forest went out. The flames died down on the heads of the deer as they picked their way gently over the crust of snow into the depths of the forest. The rabbits hopped away like dark little clumps of moss on the white, the trees stood dim and silent. Somewhere the last burning snowflake shone up like a little drop of red blood before its light flickered and went out.

High above the valley rode the moon over clear cold skies. Its silver light poured down into the ravines and snow-filled crevices of the mountains and played upon the icy pool beneath the peaks, touching the dark trees in the forest with its pale light and passing over the valley in the silent night.

THE CHILD ON THE PATH

A long, long time ago, two brothers, Beno and Ivel, set out one winter's noon from a busy market town where they both lived to cross the mountains into the valley beyond where their old mother lived in a lonely little cottage. For no greater joy did the old woman have than to see her two sons once a year, as at other times they were too busy to make the long journey on foot.

It was their wont to leave their work at noon on Christmas Eve. They would then walk the whole afternoon and part of the night to come down on the other side of the mountain just as the bells began to ring for the midnight service in the little church in the village where their mother lived and where they were born. And there she would be, coming along with the other villagers in a silent procession through the snow. Her sons joined her at the point where the mountain path opened up onto the square in front of the church, and together they entered the warmth within and celebrated the birth of Him Who is the Lord of All.

Afterwards came the greetings of the village folk and the twelve joyful days with their mother in her warm little house—then the leave-taking and the journey up over the mountains back to the market town for another year.

Beno and Ivel were good sons and devout men and not much more can be said of them except that Beno was the more wilful and Ivel somewhat quiet.

The sky was clear and blue albeit the sun's orb hung low, for it was just past the shortest day in the year. The air was frosty as if mingled with finely ground glass. Beno and Ivel were well buttoned up in sheepskin jackets and on their feet they wore thick boots. Each carried a bundle of gifts for their mother and food for the long walk.

Away ahead rose the mountain ridge over the crest of which wound their path. At the foot of the mountain, silent in the gathering shadows of the winter's afternoon lay a dark pine forest, its tall sombre trees pointing upwards towards the snow-covered mountain peaks. The ascent to the ridge lay through the forest which the brothers knew well in its friendliness as well as its dangers, for although the path rose easily towards the heights through the straight tall trees standing in the snow, steep slopes fell away from the path further up and great care was needed to reach the crest safely.

Beno and Ivel trudged on over the fields towards the forest, leaving the market town wrapped in frosty mist behind. The mountain loomed nearer, the blue of the sky was fast deepening and the brothers, sometimes silent, sometimes talkative, were both full of that tingling expectancy a man feels when the Holy Nights draws near and he is soon to see his mother again.

A tiny figure was on the path ahead of them. As they went on, the distance between them and the dark little figure grew less and less and soon they caught up with it. It was a little child, poorly clad with a pinched and drawn face and great dark eyes full of distress. The child looked up at the brothers as they made to pass by and its look of deep sorrow stayed their feet.

"Can we do anything for you, little one?" asked Ivel.

"Are you two going over the mountain?" the child asked in a thin clear voice.

"Aye, we are," said Ivel.

"Then take me with you; my mother has lost me and I must find her tonight."

Ivel and Beno took the child between them, each holding one thin cold hand and on they went.

Night fell and on the indigo sky above shone the thousandfold silver lights of heaven and the air prickled with frost. As the brothers went on up with the child between them, they felt its hands grow heavier. Indeed after a time, it seemed as though they were dragging a load as heavy as the world. Beno began to grumble for they had proceeded only very slowly since meeting the child and had not covered the distance they should have done to reach the other side of the mountain before midnight. Ivel was silent and pondered on the strangeness of the child who though so slight of frame was so leaden of weight.

After a long time, they reached the edge of the forest and entered its cold stillness. The child was heavier than ever as they began the steep ascent to the ridge and hot tears of wrath sprang into Beno's eyes as he looked up and saw by the position of the stars that the hour of midnight was not far off.

"It is bad enough that we shall not see our mother tonight and that she will think that calamity has befallen us. Indeed calamity has befallen us, for what can be worse than not to receive the blessing on the Lord's Night? And all because of this miserable child who has held us up!"

Ivel was silent and the child too, but if its weight could have sounded, the stillness of the forest would have been broken by a mighty noise.

Slowly, interminably slowly, they reached the edge of the forest and above them the icy ridge of the mountain stood out against the midnight sky.

Suddenly Beno broke loose from the child and his brother: "I can bear it no longer. If you will, Ivel, then stay with this wretched child, but I cannot let our mother wait nor do I want to miss the priest's blessing lest I lose my eternal life. I am leaving you!"

"Do so, Beno," said Ivel, "and give our mother my greetings. I shall be with you in the morning."

Beno now free from his burden hurried on ahead. He soon reached the ridge and took his way down the other side of the mountain along the path that led into the little village where his mother lived. When he arrived, everything was dark; not a single light shone, for the Holy Hour was past and all the village folk were asleep. Beno went through the silent little village to his mother's cottage and roused her through his knocking.

"Where have you left Ivel"? she asked straightway when she saw him standing alone in the doorway.

Beno told his mother what had happened.

"You have done wrongly to have left Ivel and the child behind. You should go back for them for surely the child needs help." His mother's voice was full of strange displeasure. Shame burned in Beno's cheeks as he turned back to search for Ivel.

Ivel watched Beno's broad figure stamp through the snow on the path as he mounted ever higher until he stood for a moment on the top of the ridge before he dropped out of sight. The small hand in his was cold. Peering into the face of the child by the light of the stars reflected on the snow, Ivel saw that it was white and drawn. "Come, little one," he

said, "I have something to eat in my pack and see, here is my warm jacket to put around you."

Ivel took off his jacket and wrapped it around the child, ashamed that he had not thought of doing so before. Sitting down on a rock under the silent trees, he took the little child on his knees and fed him with bread from his store. Strange, he thought, the child weighs no more than a bundle of fleece.

It was cold and Ivel tried not to shiver. He held the little child closely and felt his silken hair brush his cheek. He was weary and cold, but his heart was light.

Up on the ridge of the mountain there was a light. Ivel wondered who would be crossing at this hour. Nearer and nearer came the light. Now it was a soft warm glow and was coming his way. Ivel watched the glow approach and all at once he saw what it was.

A woman walked swiftly over the snow and as her blue cloak trailed behind her, the snow crystals burst into flame and glowed like a thicket of roses all down the mountainside. The woman's face was grave and her lovely eyes were searching. Ivel rose and went to meet her.

"Have you lost your child?" he asked and held out the little child to the woman. She took the child from Ivel into the blue of her cloak. She did not say a word, but before she turned to go her fiery way over the snow, she laughed for joy. It was like the silver ringing of an unearthly bell wrought out of molten love. The sound trickled into Ivel's heart and mingled with his blood.

He stood and watched the woman go until the last little flame died down behind her. Then he picked up his bundle and went on up over the crest of the mountain in the light of the dawn.

Beno saw Ivel, his brother, coming down the winding path with a light step, his bundle slung over his shoulder. He was wearing no jacket and the child too was gone. Beno hurried to meet him but stopped suddenly when he saw the look on his brother's face.

"What has happened?" he cried.

"Nothing that need make you anxious, Beno," said Ivel softly, "I have heard the Queen of Heaven laugh and from now on, all my life will be an echo of that sound."

Then Beno and Ivel went down to their mother.

THE KING FROM THE NORTH

Far in the north, there was a land ruled over by a king who was mighty in very many ways. First and foremost he was a strong and brave warrior, leading his armies into battle, an example to his own men and to his enemies alike, and when he was clad in his heavy armour, he looked as stalwart as an oak.

When peace reigned in and around his land, the king sat on his throne arrayed in royal garments holding the sceptre and orb, the signs of kingship, exercising his power for the good of his people. The sight of him then was one of splendour and majesty and his people both honoured and obeyed him.

When high days of worship came in that kingdom and the people streamed to the temple in the centre of the city in festive reverence, it was their king who stood before the altar as the high priest of the land, clad in a robe of pure white linen, his hands raised to the gods in supplication or stretched out over the heads of his people in wise benediction.

Thus he was warrior, king and priest—all three—and when the occasion demanded, one more than the other two. Few if any knew him other than in these three capacities, yet sometimes when he was alone, he was neither warrior nor king or priest; rather a tender youth whose soul was aglow with a little flame of longing—for what, he did not know save that it was for something infinitely high and precious. He seldom had opportunity to be that tender youth, for his kingdom, being vast, demanded much of him.

It happened one night that the king had a dream of great sweetness. When he awoke, the dream faded and he could recall nothing of its content other than that he had found what he longed for in his still moments, and that finding it was inconceivable bliss.

He went about his kingly duties, but the imprint of his dream had gone deep into his soul and increased in effect from day to day. Finally the effect of his dream grew so powerful that he resolved to leave his kingdom for a while and to make a pilgrimage—whither he did not know but he trusted that a higher power would guide his steps.

He committed the care of his kingdom into the hands of his uncle, a steadfast and trustworthy man and prepared himself for the journey that lay ahead.

He rode away from his kingdom alone, clad in his armour, his shield on his left arm, his sword at his side. As a warrior he rode away into the unknown regions beyond the borders of his kingdom, but beneath his armour he wore his royal robes as well as his priestly ones.

He rode for a long time until his own kingdom lay far below the horizon. He was now in a barren rocky wilderness where no grass grew and no beast darted across his path nor did he hear any sound such as the song of birds. The rocks rose into cliffs on either side, ever steeper and the path beneath him narrowed ever more—so much so that he could not have turned his horse about had he desired to return home at that point. He rode on perforce and the cliffs closed in upon him scraping his shield and his sword stuck in the crevices of the rock hindering his progress. All at once, the jutting rocks caught his shield so that it buckled as it hung on his arm and he could do nothing but free himself from the useless thing and cast it away behind him. As he did so, his sword jammed rudely in the walls of the cliff. He had no leeway to pull it out, so he edged on slowly, leaving his sword where it was.

Now the gorge had narrowed so that the rocks almost closed in over his head shutting out the grey daylight. His brave horse heaved great sighs as it tried to forge its way ahead but soon its heaving and pushing were of no avail, for the passage had become too narrow for a beast of that size or for any beast for that matter. The king slipped over his horse's head and edged it backwards until it was somewhat free of the trap in which it had been caught, and then he signed to it to make its way back out of the gorge as best it could.

He himself went on but he could make little headway for now his armour prevented his passage through the gorge. He divested himself of his armour piece by piece, leaving it on the path behind him, and now stood in his royal robe of purple, a delicate band of gold on his brow. Thus he forced himself through the narrowest part of the gorge.

Once through, he came out into a widening valley with a broad path before him. The sun shone on his kingly splendour and the few wayfarers who passed by were awe-struck to see a king walking unaccompanied by any man or servant, but no one was so bold as to address him.

After a time, he heard the sound of waves breaking upon shores and ahead he saw a wide ocean stretching out into the distance. Unerringly the king went on knowing that his search must continue whatever the obstacles that lay on his way. When he reached the seashore, he plunged into the wild waves in all his splendid array and with powerful strokes he began to swim.

The sky above was dark, the waters around were cold and his garments were heavy with brine. His purple robe flapped about his limbs entwining them and drawing him under. Bit by bit as he swam on, he freed himself of his royal robes leaving them to the play of the waves and his golden crown sank to the bottom of the sea.

After a long time, he reached the shores of a distant land and weary, he stepped out of the waves onto the sands clad only in his priestly vestment of simple white linen.

Before him stretched a great plain gleaming in the moonlight. Here and there a knoll rose or a dell fell away under his feet as he strode on. A wind began to blow over the plain—softly at first, sighing among the tufts of grass, but then growing stronger and steadier until it became a gale that swept the clouds over the face of the moon and whipped up the dust on the plain. The king bowed his head and shoulders to the force of the wild wind which lashed his priest's garment in tiny shreds from his body. Each shred that was torn away in the howling storm caused exquisite pain as though his very skin were being ripped off his flesh, while the flying dust stung his eyes to blindness. What he did not see therefore was the bright glow ahead, so bright that it was like the sun itself at midnight. It shone out from a little Child lying on its mother's knee. This was the well of light sprung up in the darkness of the earth, shining up into the universe, shining out onto the rapt faces of the men who knelt in silence in that place, simple men who were shepherds of the flocks that graze out on the hills under the stars at night; and wiser men knelt there as well, three noble sovereigns, one from morning, one from midday and one from the land where the sun sets—all come to drink from the well-spring of Love.

The king from the land of the north which the sun passes by, blinded, torn by the cruel gale, divested of all his signs of strength, royalty and sanctity, reached the silent circle too. He took his place among the adoring kings and shepherds as the tender youth whose dream had led him here, yet not as you would think—as a youth for all to see—but as a little flame of fire hovering tenderly, inwardly above the Child in whose wonderful eyes the fiery little flame was knowingly reflected.

The Christmas Rose

A pilgrim came down from a mountain pass onto the wide plain of a valley. Snow lay deep on his way—with each step he sank into its white softness. The branches of the fir trees weighed down by snow trailed their long finger-like tips over the drifts beneath them and the moon shone cold and clear upon the white plain. Stillness reigned, broken only by the sound of the pilgrim trudging through the snow.

Ahead of him lay a city like a dark shadow on the moonlit whiteness of the plain. A few lights twinkled from within the shadow but their lights were outshone by the stars above which gleamed so brilliantly that the pilgrim almost heard them resound. He felt weary as he trudged on towards the city for a long, hard way lay behind him. The moon was riding high and he knew that the hour was late and concern assailed him lest he fail to find a place to spend the night.

On he went and now the heavy walls of the city loomed up before him, blocking out the white hills in the distance. The pilgrim turned his steps towards the great gate marked by two massive towers. Lights burned in the tower windows and the pilgrim perceived that the gates were still open. A sense of relief flooded through his veins at the thought that he would soon be warming himself at a hearth and breaking bread and afterwards resting from the toilsome day behind him.

He came to the narrow arched stone bridge that spanned the moat around the city walls, and set foot on the bridge, longing to escape from the silvery coldness of the open plain. Scarcely had he crossed the bridge when two watchmen came out of the towers and swung the iron gates of the city together. He cried out and ran towards the gates, but when he had reached them they were securely bolted and the watchmen had gone. One by one the lights in the towers went out and now the cold bright moonlight crept up to the city walls and reigned over all. The pilgrim leaned against the gate pulling his cloak around his body, for an icy breath of air had begun to stir in and out of the ramparts. Despair possessed his heart for he was hungry, cold and very weary.

All at once he heard a child cry. Looking up he saw a woman standing on the bridge with a young child on her arm. The pilgrim hurried towards her: "Woman, why is your child crying? Have you too been shut out of the city?" "Shut gates do not matter to us," said the woman "but my child has lost his plaything and cannot be comforted." "Then let me look for it," said the pilgrim, "and if I find it, your child will be glad again. Where can he have lost it?" The woman pointed to the black water in the moat below. "There it floats," she said, "but it will be difficult to get."

The pilgrim looked down and in the light of the moon, he saw a little object on the surface of the water but could not discern its nature. To the weeping child on its mother's arm, he said: "I shall fetch it for you."

Casting his cloak off his shoulders, the pilgrim pulled up his nether garment and climbed down under the bridge to the edge of the moat. The plaything was still floating on the water. Peering at it in the moonlight, he was almost certain it was a red rose. He broke a twig from a nearby bush and reached out cautiously, but he slipped and plunged full length into the cold black water. He straightaway found his footing for the water was not deeper than up to his breast, but the ripples caused by his plunge had washed the little object a good way ahead. He still heard the little child weeping on the bridge although he saw neither him nor his mother. So wading slowly in the icy water, he went after the lost plaything.

The city walls now took a sharp bend and cast their massive shadow over the moat. The pilgrim lost sight of the little object, yet sometimes it appeared to be in front of him, sometimes to his left, sometimes to his right, but it was colourless and elusive or it might have been but the fitful play of the moonlight among the shadows.

The pilgrim was cold to the marrow of his bones. The black water seemed to break in on him and flood through his inner being... Suddenly the moat came to an end and just above the pilgrim was an ancient copper door and on it engraved but scarcely discernible were the twelve starry signs of heaven. In spite of the gathering darkness within him, he perceived them clearly and took this to be the door of death. Heaving himself out of the water, he grasped hold of the handle of the door which opened. He found himself in a long winding passage leading gently downwards. There was no light in the passage yet the pilgrim walked unerringly: Is there something other than light that can make one see, he thought?

At last the passage came to an end in a rounded vault which he could perceive quite clearly. In the middle of the vault lay three dead kings. That they were kings the pilgrim could tell because of the crowns on their heads and the sceptres at their sides. They were awe-some and beautiful in death, each covered to the breast in a shroud—the first one red, the second one blue and the third one green.

Suddenly a door burst open and in a blaze of light, a multitude of knights and pages carrying torches entered the vault. Two sovereigns went among them, one wearing ruby coloured robes and a high bejeweled crown on his head, the other in dull gold with a blunt crown glinting with many precious metals and stones.

The pilgrim was startled by this splendid company and receded into the shadows hoping not to be seen.

Now the two sovereigns came forward and knelt before the catafalques and their knights and pages knelt behind them. They began to pray loudly, invoking the dead kings to increase the glory and the power of their thrones in the eyes of all men.

The pilgrim was troubled and thought: What have I to do in a place where kings worship? In that moment, the three dead kings began to stir. One by one they rose from their stony couches, their shrouds falling to the ground. The two sovereigns and their company were struck with terror to see the dead astir, but the pilgrim felt his heart expand with awe—never had he witnessed anything so majestic and noble as the rising of the three kings.

When the three kings had taken their sceptres into their hands, the king who had the red shroud began to speak: "We have risen from the state of death because there is one here in this vault who has a sign that calls us back to earth."

"We serve him whose sign it is," said the blue-shrouded king, "and whoever wears it, him too shall we serve."

The green king signed to the two sovereigns to rise to their feet: "Have no fear; to him who has the sign we shall give our blessing. To him who does not have it we shall bring no harm."

The terror that had gripped the two sovereigns and their followers now melted away and each thought that perhaps he was the bearer of the sign that had awakened the three kings and they all stood waiting for the name of the one to be called, but the three kings, although sensing the presence of the sign, did not find it amongst the bright company assembled in the vault. All at once, the green king saw the pilgrim standing in the shadows and he called out in a ringing voice: "There is the one who has the sign!"

The company parted to make way for the pilgrim to come forward. "See," said the red king, "on your breast you are wearing the sign that has called us to life!"

The pilgrim looked down on himself; there on his rough brown garment, caught by its thorns, hung a red rose. He closed his eyes to the brightness around him and knelt before the three kings. Into his mind there streamed a golden light, into his heart a sweet glow and into his limbs an unknown strength.

When he rose to his feet, the vault, the three dead kings, the bright company had vanished and he found himself in a vast cathedral filled with people. Sunlight shone in through the many-coloured windows. In the spires the bells were ringing out the jubilance of a Christmas morning and a choir of many hundreds of voices filled the lofty spaces with music.

As the pilgrim passed through the crowds, he was greeted silently but joyously by one and the other among them. In the eyes of those who greeted him, he saw the eyes of the little Child on the bridge and he knew that he had his rose again.

A CHILD'S CHRISTMAS

A Kind of Fairy Tale

Christmas was drawing near. The nights lay over the days like dark spangled hoods although not many in the great city noticed the stars of the night because the street lights and the lights that poured from the shop windows outshone what was above.

One afternoon when it was just getting dark, a small child walked along at the side of a kind person who was going to give the child a Christmas treat. They rounded a corner into a big, bright street jammed with buses and cars and people hurrying in all directions. High up over the street, garlands of coloured electric lights flashed on and off; one moment you saw this and the next moment that and then again this and afterwards that—in silent jerky rhythms, telling everyone what was best to buy.

But all these lights and more were not enough to eclipse the row of lit-up Christmas trees perched along the vast ledge of a huge square building. The kind person said to the child: "Look, how lovely"! The child blinked at the brownish-orange electric bulbs hanging on all the trees, so many of them. Between the trees, there were as many enormous heads with bulbous cheeks, benignly glaring down into the street. "Who's that?" asked the child. "Santa Claus," said the kind person.

They crossed the big street which was like crossing a rushing torrent and headed straight for the huge square building that had many doors that swung to and fro all the time to let the crowding people carrying boxes and parcels in and out and in. The kind person and the child entered the shop and the tightly packed lift and went up and up to the "Kiddies Dreamland"—the toy department.

"Isn't it lovely?" exclaimed the kind person. The child looked and saw rows and rows of dinky cars, plastic toys, dolls, fluffy dogs with ribbons, Mickey Mouses and teddy bears. From all corners came squawking noises, some from rocking dolls and others from raucous trumpets blown by other children and there was a constant undertone of tinny melodies all playing at the same time. Near the child was a counter full of big shiny pistols and black tanks, and in the midst of everything a man dressed in red all over, with a red hood and a long white cotton-wool beard, nodding his head at all the kiddies. "Who's that?" asked the child. "That's Santa Claus," said the kind person. The child caught sight of another counter where there were rows and rows of tiny fat plastic men dressed in red all over with red hoods and long white cotton-wool beards.

The young child had not learned to think yet like grown-ups; she only believed. She believed that in the Christmas Night, a Spirit unlike anything else on earth, knowing and warm and pure, came into your room, unseen and unheard, but felt because it was full of Grace that filled your heart. His sign was all the lovely presents that Mother laid for you under the Tree—not too many but each one precious. Grown-ups seemed to call that spirit—Santa Claus. The child did not mind the name because it did not know a better one.

But on this afternoon, there were Santa Clauses everywhere, live ones and not live ones as if someone were making a joke that drew no smile. Something began to break very softly inside the young child and that was her power to stand in awe in the face of wonder. The child grew paler and paler, but there was still another Santa Claus to be met—the real one who sat in a tent which you could enter if your grown-up paid—holding a big, big bag between his knees from which you were allowed to choose something. The child was a little shy and did not choose right away, so the Santa Claus put a grimy hand into the bag and drew out a plastic panda and gave it to the child who was not quite sure if it was meant as a gift or not.

"Now," said the kind person "We'll go to the pictures; there's something lovely on for kiddies."

The child had a seat of her own in the huge dim room, but could not see over the heads of the people in front, so she sat on the kind person's knee.

There was something about a Christmas Eve dinner prepared for Mickey Mouse. The child could not quite grasp what the shaky voices that came from somewhere had to do with the violently flickering sheet of disjointed pictures in front, but the kind person explained that the big bad cat had come to gobble up Mickey's Christmas dinner, and now Mickey Mouse was flinging all the food in the cat's face and whizzing here and whizzing there, making everyone roar with laughter.

Finally the noise and the flickering stopped and the lights in the big room went on; the child followed the kind person out into the street.

The kind person was going to complete the Christmas treat by taking the child to a Christmas party. First of all, the child had to go home and be changed into a nylon party dress the kind person had given her while the kind person herself waited downstairs.

They then set out again. When they arrived at the house where the party was being held, the child heard loud noises coming from within. In the room which was decorated with paper streamers and an electric bulb-laden tree, there were lots of children. They were jumping up at a large fat Santa Claus and pulling at his beard and squealing with laughter. The Santa Claus defended himself by handing out crackers and as soon as each child got his cracker, he pulled it with a loud bang and unwrapped the tissue paper cap inside and either put it on or threw it on the floor because he had so many already.

For a moment, the young child believed that this Santa Claus was real because he was so round and benign. The child was led to him for a cracker and caught a glimpse of the eyes in his round face. Something in them made the child very frightened; the grown-ups call it—boredom.

The party went on and got louder and louder. The grown-ups, always smiling and kind, went round with cakes and sweets and bottles of pop, until you were dizzy from over-eating, but when they came round again, you could not stop your hand from reaching out and taking more.

Finally, the treat of the evening was announced and the children were led into the big, dim drawing-room where they sat down on the thick carpet and began to watch. A box that was lit up inside stood on a small table in the corner. It showed little men chasing around a field kicking a ball so hard that the child was afraid it would be hurt. From time to time, there were loud roars from somewhere in the room.

Then something in the box changed and you saw some men riding on horses very fast. All at once, they turned around and shot—bang! The child was terrified because it thought that someone in the room must be hurt. Bang-bang-bang! The child was sick on the floor. A not quite so kind person took the child home.

Far above the sleeping troubled child, far above all sleeping and troubled children, up there where the stars speak their silent speech no longer heard on earth—the souls of the children of the great city gather, rising above the hubbub and haste of the brilliantly illumined grown-up world so full of wants, to commune with their angels in the manner of the souls of children at night.

And so our child communed with her angel: O my angel, my soul has been lacerated by kind people who showed me the mass production of things I thought were only once, who showed me beastly caricatures of animals I love when all I longed to see was a Golden Child in the night. My soul has been bruised by multitudinous flashes, when I yearned for a little Light shining all alone in the darkness. My soul has been torn by noises and bangs when I hoped to hear a still small voice whispering one single word. O my angel, it is hard to bear the many many things heaped up in the world when all I want is a humble toy which for a while takes the place of a friend and listens to the tales I tell it.

And I have further trouble, O my angel, because one day I'll be a grown-up too and with a smiling face, I'll lacerate the souls of as yet unborn children who long to believe, to wonder, to hope, and who know that there is a magic Spirit among the stars Who sees into your soul and answers hidden prayers, because I will have forgotten what it is like to be a child. O my angel, I am troubled.

The angel spoke in a voice like rushing waters: Child! the Lord Christ will not allow all children to grow up and forget. He will see that some remain simple and untouched by the senselessness of the grown-up world, even when they become adult. Some people will say that they are strange and perhaps backward, because they will be free from the haste and wants that beset so many lives. But in spite of what people will say, these children will be capable of much more than others and will be able to lead and to help because they will believe, and to believe is not what the grown-ups think it is—to have 'mere blind faith'. Faith and belief are not blind—they are the high knowledge of the heart that there is a living Divine Reality in and around all men, although most would not have it so or are unaware of it.

These special children will keep that knowledge alive. But you, my child, are one of the countless suffering ones of the world in whom real joy is almost blotted out… The angel wrapped his wings around the soul of the sleeping child for a while in the night, until dawn came and it had to go back to the world below.

Easter

THE STONE OF PATIENCE

There was once a woman who lived with her daughter in a little hut at the foot of the Great Mountains. One day as she sat spinning with her daughter, she said: "My child, you are coming into the years when you should no longer be sitting at my side spinning, but should be walking at the side of your bridegroom." The maiden sighed and answered: "Mother, no man ever comes past this way and besides—what man would take a maiden as poor as I am?" "But you are fair, my child," said the woman, "not only of face but of soul as well." And they went on spinning.

One day very early in the spring, the woman paused in her spinning and listened: "Child, the wild swans are flying! Run out and listen to their tidings!"

The maiden went outside and saw the wild swans flying overhead: "Wild swans, wild swans, do you bring tidings?" But the wild swans flew on until they were gone behind the mountains.

A few days later, the woman paused again in her spinning: "Child, the wild geese are flying! Run out and listen to their tidings!" The maiden went out and saw the wild geese flying overhead: "Wild geese, wild geese, do you bring tidings?" But the wild geese flew on until they were gone behind the mountains.

A few days later, the woman paused in her spinning: "Child, the raven, the Bird of Sorrow, is croaking outside by the doorpost." The maiden arose: "Mother, I will go outside and listen to what he says."

She went out and found the raven sitting by the doorpost: "Bird of Sorrow, do you bring tidings?" The raven answered: "Fair maid, I bring tidings of your bridegroom." "Who is he and when is he coming?" asked the maiden. "He is the Prince who lies dead in the Mountain and no other," croaked the raven and flew away. The maiden went in to her mother. "What did the raven say?" asked the woman. The maiden answered: "He said that my bridegroom was the Prince who lies dead in the Mountain and no other." And she sat down and wept.

The woman arose and said: "Never seek to alter Fate when it comes, my daughter. You will have to go in search of the Prince who lies dead in the Mountain. Come, arise and I shall go with you."

So the woman and her daughter made ready to go. They took baskets with bread and their staffs. Before they left the hut, the woman made the Lord's Sign over the place where they lived and then they set out into the forest.

As they went they picked fresh herbs that grew by the wayside. All at once, the woman stopped and picked a herb and gave it to her daughter: "It is Sweet Basil, the Herb of Golgotha, my child. It grew along the path Our Lord trod as He mounted the hill to the Cross. Keep it and it will bring you blessing." The maiden put the Herb of Golgotha in her bosom. As they went deeper and deeper into the forest, it grew darker and a storm arose. The woman and her daughter saw a cave in the mountainside and were going to take shelter there when a mighty flash of lightning blinded them in the roaring thunder. When everything was still again the maiden had vanished. "My daughter, my daughter," cried the mother, "where are you?"

Inside the Mountain, the maiden came into a room in which a candle was burning, but the room was empty.

She went into the next room. There was a candle burning in it, but the room was empty. She went into a third room—but there was no one there. On and on the maiden went into thirty-nine rooms, but she found no one in any of them.

At last she came into the fortieth room. There lay a dead Prince with a candle burning at his head and one at his feet. His hands were crossed on his breast and in them was a scroll with writing on it.

The maiden gazed on the dead Prince and knew that this was her bridegroom. All at once into the room came an ancient hag: "Ah, my fair maiden," she screeched, "have you found your way into the Mountain where the dead Prince lies? Then draw forth the scroll from his hands and read what is written on it out loud to me." For the hag knew that the scroll contained words of life that could raise the soul of the Prince. She could not read them herself but was waiting for someone to come and read them to her—for she wanted to wed the dead Prince and have him as her own.

The maiden drew the scroll out of the dead Prince's hand and unrolled it. The ancient hag bent over her shoulder: "Read it, read it," she croaked, "what does it say?"

"It is not light enough," said the maiden.

"Come over to the candle," said the hag, and pushed the maiden forward. "The writing is too small," said the maiden. "Then look closer, look closer," said the hag and thrust the maiden's head over the writing.

For in truth the writing said: Maiden, these are words for you alone. You shall be my bride if you have enough endurance. Burn incense at my head for full forty days and nights and keep watch all the while and all will be well. But see to it that you do not fail for this will mean great sorrow for us both.

"What does it say?" croaked the hag.

The maiden rolled up the scroll and put it in her basket: "It says that incense must be burned at the head of the dead Prince against his burial." "Aha," said the hag, "then you can do that!" and she left the maiden alone with the Prince.

The maiden took up a bowl of incense and lit it and sat down at the Prince's head and the sweet smoke rose upwards.

Day after day and night after night, the maiden burned incense, filling the bowl when it was empty.

When many days and nights had passed the ancient hag entered the room. She did not believe that the maiden was burning incense against the burial of the dead Prince but against his rising.

She went up to the maiden: "Fair maid, how much longer must you burn incense? Surely he should have been buried long since!"

"That is not for me to say," said the maiden.

"Then let me burn incense for a while so that you may rest," croaked the hag, and tried to snatch the bowl out of the maiden's hands.

But the maiden held out the sprig of the Herb of Golgotha and the hag had no power against it.

After many more days and nights had passed, the hag again entered the room. She went up to the maiden and said: "Fair maid, how much longer must you burn incense? Surely he should have been buried long since!"

"That is not for me to say," said the maiden.

"Then let me burn incense for a while so that you may rest," croaked the hag and tried to snatch the bowl out of the maiden's hand, but the maiden held out the sprig of the Herb of Golgotha and the hag had no power against it.

Three nights before the dawn of the fortieth day of burning incense at the head of the dead Prince, the maiden felt an ocean of weariness within her. Her eyelids were heavy and her head fell forward onto her breast, but she pulled it up with a jerk.

A second time her eyelids were heavy and her head fell forward onto her breast but she pulled it up with a jerk.

A third time her eyelids were heavy and her head fell forward onto her breast and the maiden slept.

At this moment the hag entered the room and seeing the maiden asleep, stole up and drew the bowl of incense from her lap, thrust the maiden off the stool and sat down at the head of the dead Prince.

The maiden awoke from her fall and seeing the hag sitting in her place, she wept bitterly.

The hag laughed and said: "Aha, fair maid, you thought he would be yours, but he is going to be mine! You shall be my servant. Go out into the forest and find a spring of cold water and bring me some to drink that I may stay awake tonight."

The maiden took a jug and went out into the forest. As she searched for the spring, she saw two men in black carrying a Knife between them.

"What is that you are carrying?" asked the maiden. "It is the Knife of Slaughter," answered the two men. The maiden said to the Knife of Slaughter: "What shall I do, O Knife of Slaughter?"

The Knife answered: "Slay yourself, lady." The maiden took up the Knife, but the Herb of Golgotha at her bosom whispered: "Wait!" And the two men went on. The maiden drew water from the spring and took it back to the hag.

The next day the hag said to the maiden: "Go out into the forest and draw cold water from the spring and bring me some to drink that I may stay awake tonight."

The maiden took a jug and went out into the forest. As she searched for the spring, she saw two men in grey carrying a Rope.

"What is that you are carrying?" asked the maiden. "It is the Rope of Hanging," said the two men. The maiden said to the Rope of Hanging: "What shall I do, O Rope of Hanging?" The Rope answered: "Hang yourself, lady." The maiden took up the Rope, but the Herb of Golgotha at her bosom whispered: "Wait!" And the two men went on.

On the third day the hag said to the maiden: "Go out into the forest and draw cold water from the spring and bring me some to drink that I may stay awake tonight."

The maiden took a jug and went out into the forest. As she searched for the spring, she saw two men in brown carrying a Stone between them. "What is that you are carrying?" asked the maiden. "It is the Stone of Patience," said the two men. The maiden said to the Stone: "What shall I do, O Stone of Patience?" The Stone answered: "Wear me around your neck, lady." The Herb of Golgotha at her breast whispered: "Do as the Stone tells you." The maiden took the Stone of Patience and hung it around her neck and the two men went on. She filled her jug and took it back to the hag.

When evening came, the hag said to the maiden: "Because tomorrow is my wedding day, I will grant you a wish." "Then let me go out and sit by the doorpost," said the maiden. She went outside and fell on her knees by the doorpost and with the Stone of Patience hanging heavily around her neck, she spent the night in prayer.

Early in the morning just before dawn, the end of the forty days had come. The dead Prince rose from his sleep and stood upon his feet. When he raised his eyes and saw the hag sitting at the head of the bier and the maiden kneeling by the doorpost outside, he cried out: "Which of you is my rightful bride?"

"I am, I am," croaked the hag and took his hand, "for it was I and no other who burned incense at your head these full forty days and nights." "And who is that maiden?" cried the Prince. "She is my servant," answered the hag. The Prince went and stood beside the kneeling maiden and saw the Stone of Patience hanging around her neck. Then he said to the hag: "If you are my rightful bride, you will be wearing the most Precious Jewel around your neck. Show me the sign!"

"I can show you," screeched the hag and flung back her cloak. On her breast hung many a jewel she had stolen and hoarded in the

Mountain. But the Prince took the maiden by the hand and raised her to her feet: "What is that you are wearing on your breast, fair maiden?" he asked. "It is the Stone of Patience, sire," she said. "The Stone of Patience," cried the Prince, "is the most Precious Jewel and she who wears it is my bride and no other!"

But the ancient hag in black wrath stole up behind the Prince and was going to wrest him away from the maiden by evil spells. The maiden saw her and held out the sprig of the Herb of Golgotha and cried: "Do not touch him, wicked hag. He shall be free!" The hag shrivelled up and fell in a heap on the ground and the spell was lifted from the Prince.

The maiden said to her bridegroom: "Come, my mother is waiting in the house."

So hand in hand, they went through the forest until they saw the hut where the woman sat by her spinning wheel thinking of her lost daughter.

Suddenly she heard a sound and looking up she saw the two standing by the doorpost and great was the joy between them from that day to this.

THE KING AND HIS PAGE

A king and his page rode one spring day through a forest. The air was still and soft and sweet with the smell of fresh earth. They met no one in the forest as they rode and silence reigned between them, for the king was oppressed by doubts and darknesses of spirit too heavy to be shared with so young a page. The latter rode behind his master, his sharp eyes concerned with keeping to the path which was not easy—for few rode that way, and the thicket took possession of the traces made by any rider the moment he passed by.

When evening came and the mottled sunlight shone rosy into the forest glades, the king and his page had not reached the far edge of the forest whither they were riding; indeed they seemed to be still in the heart of it and saw no sign of life other than that of the wood and its creatures. By and by they rode into a little clearing carpeted with soft young grass at the foot of a hill over which the great forest heaved itself. At the edge of the clearing there ran a little brook, its busy waters seeking their course through reedy grasses and over stones and around little bends. "Let us rest here for the night," said the king "it is mild and this place is well sheltered."

The page set about preparing an evening meal for his master after leading the horses to drink and tending them and tethering them within reach of the succulent grass. Soon all was ready and king and page had their meal in the clearing, while the daylight faded gently and the only sounds were of the horses cropping and the brook gurgling and the occasional cry of a night bird far off in the forest.

"I am weary," said the king to his page, "and I wish to sleep. See that you keep watch during the night so that no harm befall us."

The king drew his sword from its sheath and laid it on the grass. He wrapped himself in his cloak and lay down beside it and soon he was asleep.

The page looked again to the horses, then cleared away the remains of the meal. When all was tidy, he went and sat down near his master and listened to his deep breathing and to the other soft sounds of the night. Through the treetops on the hill shone the rising moon, its silver light seeking ways along the twigs and trunks of the trees, slipping down into the depths of the forest, alighting on the waters of the brook and gliding over the dark clumps of moss.

Higher and higher rose the spring moon and now its full brightness poured down into the clearing and the page could see the features of his master distinctly. As he gazed on them, he saw a tiny golden serpent slip out of the king's mouth. For a moment it paused on his lips seeming to seek its direction, then it slid down swiftly over the king's body onto the turf below. The page watched it slither through the grass, its slender golden body catching the silver light of the moon as it made its way towards the brook. The page rose softly to his feet and followed the little serpent. It was weaving its way back and forth at the edge of the stream, seeking to cross over, but each time it crept onto a stone, it turned back for fear of the bubbling water. For a time, the page watched its anxious endeavours, then he softly picked up his master's sword from the place where it lay and carrying it to the brook, laid it across the water, its point to the other side. The little serpent glided out of the reeds and crossed the brook along the shining blade of the sword. On the far side, it made its way up the hill; the page saw its golden body glinting faintly in the moonlight. Then it vanished.

He took up the sword and returned it to its place beside the sleeping king and sat down again to keep watch. The moon and the stars moved steadily along their nightly courses; dew fell and the page shivered for cold and wakefulness.

After many hours, the stars began to pale and one by one they vanished from sight. The moon, grown transparent, slipped away beyond the forest; the grey light that reigns between the night and the dawn filled the young page's eyes with a dull pain. Stiffly he rose to his feet and looked at the grey outlines of trees and rocks around him. All at once on the far side of the brook, he caught sight of the little golden serpent winding its way hurriedly down the hill towards the brook. Restlessly it sought its bridge—the page once more took up his master's sword and stepping through the wet grass, he laid it across the brook, its point to the clearing. The little serpent crossed over the blade and swiftly threaded its way through the grass towards the sleeping king. The page picked up the sword and following the little golden serpent, saw it disappear into his master's mouth.

Laying the sword gently at the king's side, the page sat down to wait for his master to awake.

Dawn broke and out of the hush of the night came forth the song of the birds and the colours of the spring earth.

The king awoke and rose lightly to his feet. He looked very different this morning, for his brow was peaceful and his eyes were serene. The weary page rejoiced to see his master thus restored and his joy made his morning tasks the lighter, weary though he was himself.

Soon king and page were on their way again. As they rode, the king said to the page: "You would not understand but nonetheless I will tell you something, for my heart is overflowing this morning. Until yesterday my soul was sore and weighed down by doubts that robbed me of the desire to live and that darkened my deeds. But last night as I slept in the clearing, it was as if my soul had reached the brink of a yawning chasm which it yearned to cross but could not for lack of strength. Then some strange unknown hand helped me over the chasm and on the other side, I found myself in a garden in the midst of which there lay a stone. Whether it was a tomb or a well, I cannot say—perhaps it was both. I met the Gardener by that stone; in either hand he carried a red rose and there were three at his side in his girdle. He looked at me silently for a while and then said: 'Peace be with you. Blessed are they in whom doubt can be overcome, for doubt is of the nature of shadow and there can be no shadow where there is no light. But light is first and after it comes all else. To believe is to look beyond the shadow towards the light from which the shadow proceeds.'"

"The roses in the Gardener's hands and at his side began to glow as he spoke and warmth and life and love poured forth from them into the depths of my soul. When the Gardener had vanished from my sight, I knew that in Him I had seen the light of which he had spoken, the light of the Risen One."

"Then," said the king, "I left the garden and returned to the chasm which separates the world beyond from this. Again I was powerless to cross over and I was assailed by a new fear—the fear of remaining on the other side which would have meant—my death. But that same unknown hand helped me to return to this world. Maybe that hand belonged to a servant sent by the Gardener? Who can tell?"

King and page rode on in silence.

A SPRING TALE

Once there was a young queen who reigned over a fair kingdom. Her name was Thea and she was truly queenly, being cool and proud besides being as beautiful as the transparent moon in the early morning. She conducted the affairs of her kingdom and shed her light upon all matters of state, were they of law and justice, warfare or trade, of the soil or of the arts like a planet riding aloft above the earth. Beauty and order held sway in her kingdom, yet an old prophecy spoke dark words concerning her in a riddle that no one could comprehend. Some thought they meant that the young queen would die early, but few people liked to speak of the prophecy thinking that should it be forgotten, it would lose its threat.

One spring when the dawn broke and the flowers breathed out their pent-up fragrance and all the birds burst into song at once, Thea rose from her bed and went to the narrow high window of her room to see the fresh dew on the grasses before anyone walked over them and to hear the morning song of the birds before the air was filled with other sounds. She was lovely as she stood there clad in white, still flushed by the pink of sleep. She was seldom seen soft and rosy and more glowing than cool, and it was because of this that men rather honoured than loved her and that no man desired to marry her.

Thea stood at the window and breathed in the sweet spring air. Like light wine it sent waves of soft warmth through her veins and a feeling of longing twinged the nerves of her heart. Into this soft sad stirring within her there fell an alien thing, for as she looked out over the greening treetops beyond the castle gardens, she caught sight of the tower which her father had built in the forest to serve as a dungeon, for he preferred to keep his prisoners at a distance. The stone walls of the tower were massive and only a very narrow path led to it through the thicket. Apart from the warden who took bread and water to whoever was imprisoned there at sunrise and at sunset, no one else ever took that path and the queen herself had never entered the forest, although the window of her room looked out towards it and the tip of the tower rising above the treetops could be seen all the year round.

Thea never let her gaze rest upon the tower nor did she allow her thoughts to dwell upon those who might be incarcerated in it, knowing only that no prisoner had been taken there during her own short reign. But today her gaze seemed heavier and her eyes, having discerned the grey stonework of the tower, looked long at it and as they did so, a wondering rose up in her as to who might be imprisoned in the tower and for what reason.

A knock came at the door and Thea's old nurse entered the room bidding her a good morning. Straightaway Thea became the queen and commanded the nurse to dress her and do up her long fair hair in coils around her head. When her silver embroidered white woollen garment fell down in folds around her body and was girdled with a cord of gold, the awareness of her royal state drew the rosyness from her cheeks and being otherwise ready, she called for her coronet of pale silver delicately worked which the old nurse set upon her head, trembling as she did so for fear of letting it fall as well as for awe of her charge.

Thea descended into the great hall of the castle to confer with her councillors and to attend to the business of the day. For the grey haired men around her, the queen was a bright star which shed its light upon the sometimes twisted knots of the affairs of state, albeit they often thought that light a little unworldly, and whereas many matters seemed simple enough in the presence of the queen, her people laboured silently under burdens that were unknown to her. Nevertheless, Thea's councillors marvelled at her wisdom and the cool clarity of her judgement. Today again she let play the virtues with which she was graced—yet she herself was inwardly restless; her thoughts kept escaping from the matters before her and her heart followed them. For the first time, the hall seemed musty and lifeless to her and the hours of council passed heavily.

At last the business was done and the queen dismissed her councillors. Alone in the hall, she went to the window and looked out once more towards the forest beyond the gardens. The grey stone tower was just visible through the trees. A bird sang. Thea left the hall

and went through the long passage. Servants sprang forward to accompany their queen but she refused their aid and called for the warden of the tower. The old man came to her as she stood beneath the stone portal of the castle. Bowing to the young queen, he begged to hear her command. “Give me the key to the tower in the forest,” she said. The warden protested: “Lady, why do you ask this of me? I cannot permit you to go there. The tower is no place for you.” “The tower is mine,” said Thea “as much as this castle and the rest of my kingdom and no one can prevent me from entering the tower if I so wish.” “Lady,” the warden answered, “the one who is imprisoned in the tower is not there through your doing. Your father, the king, left the care of him to me and his dying command was never to let you enter the tower.”

For a moment the young queen paused, but then once more demanded the key to the tower and the old warden becoming helpless under her cool gaze, loosened the key from his belt with uncertain fingers and gave it to her. "Let no one follow me," she said, "and furthermore do not tell anyone where I am going."

Thea went down the stone steps into the garden and the old warden watched her as she proceeded along the middle path into the forest beyond. The ancient prophecy concerning her rose up in his mind and fear took possession of him as he went about his duties in the castle.

The air was sweet and the forest astir with the diligent life of its creatures. Thea came upon the tower suddenly—the path having turned and led her into a glade—and much of the apprehension she had felt left her at the sight of the mottled sunlight on the grey stone of the tower's walls and birds' knowing flight in and out of the high eaves.

Thea stood for a while in the stillness and then she mounted the steps to the tower door and turned the key in the lock. The great door opened slowly and she stepped inside. The darkness inside blotted out the daylight. The great door swung to, creaking in its rusty hinges. Thea heard the seeping of water between the stones of the walls and an occasional rustling in the straw on the floor. The place had no light of its own; only the deadened daylight that entered through the few chinks in the walls, and the air was dank and heavy. She stood in the darkness not knowing whether to flee or to stay; her senses began to reel and her limbs were leaden.

All at once she heard a louder rustling in the straw and a moan from down below. Then only did she perceive that she was standing on the edge of a deep pit. She peered into the blackness beneath which slowly dissolved into shadowy greyness and revealed the dim figure of a man crouching in a corner of the pit. A startled cry escaped her causing the man to raise his head and look up. Seeing someone other than the warden in the tower, the man himself was startled and a look of wild questioning flared up in his eyes. He rose to his feet and Thea saw that he was of good build, yet gaunt and unkempt, but noble of bearing; yet there was a look of madness in his face and in his movements. She swayed slightly and her coronet caught a dull ray of daylight in its silvery structure and at the sight of it, the prisoner gave a strange cry and began to scale the walls of the pit. With a powerful grip on the stones that jutted out of the damp and slippery sides, he climbed upwards. Thea's limbs were as heavy as stone and fear hammered in her blood. The prisoner reached the top of the pit and stood towering above her. He looked wild and fierce with his darkened eyes and matted hair and his garment hanging in rags upon his body. He reached out and swept the coronet from Thea's head and like a bull roaring in an exaltation of wrath and pain he cried: "How can you come here wearing that thing on your head? Did your father not do enough to me by robbing me of my kingdom and casting me into the nameless blackness of this tower? And now his daughter comes to taunt me wearing the crown that is mine by rights!"

It seemed to Thea that she was in the throes of an evil dream; the world had become ugly and shameful and she herself as if wading in mud. A fit of trembling seized her and she shook like a leaf in the wind. Seeing her trembling, the prisoner cried: "I see that you are aware of your father's guilt, otherwise you would not stand before me covered over and over with shame and speechless. But as you have had the means to enter this place, you will have them to leave it again. Unlock the door and lead me into my kingdom, and as you go with me you can proclaim to the people that you have robbed me of my heritage and usurped my throne!"

Fear and shame passed away and the leadenness in Thea's limbs dissolved into weightlessness. She felt utter emptiness as she turned to open the door of the tower. As the great door swung open, the prisoner stepped past her into the bright daylight, but he uttered a cry of pain for the sunlight blinded his eyes and the pain caused him to reel and fall, fainting, over the stone steps to lie still on the grass at the bottom. Thea looked down upon the prisoner lying helpless at her feet, his skin grazed by the rough stone of the steps. On the grey and empty horizon of her soul, an inner sun began to rise, filling her with the warm glow of a new dawn.

She went swiftly down the steps into the glade where not far away a clear brook gurgled over its stony bed. Tearing a piece from the hem of her garment, she dipped it into the cool water and returned to the prisoner who was lying almost deathlike upon the ground. Thea sat down beside him and washed his face and the grazes on his skin with the cool cloth. He sighed deeply and stirred a little and then without opening his eyes, fell into a deep sleep, and Thea perceived how his life quickened. She herself was wakeful for the sun within her had risen to a glowing height, changing all her silvery coolness into the gold of love.

Like this the warden found them in the evening. Anxiety for his queen had made him disobedient and when she had not returned to the castle, he went to seek her in the forest. As he came upon Thea and the sleeping prisoner, the setting sun sent long shafts of deep golden light through the leaves of the trees and rosy shadows followed in the wake of the departing sun. The glade seemed hallowed with stillness and beauty.

The warden understood in a flash that the ancient prophecy concerning Thea had reached its fulfilment. She laughed softly when she saw him coming: "You were anxious for my safety. There is no need. See, you and I now have a king; you knew him well as your prisoner—now you shall know him as your master." The warden was silent and shy, but a great burden was lifted from his heart that day.

And now the slumbering man woke up fresh and new, and the look on his face was calm instead of the madness it expressed before. He rose to his feet and seeing Thea and the warden and their eyes shining with kindness, he said: "What is to happen?" Thea answered: "You must now begin your reign and I shall serve you gladly; the warden is our dear and faithful witness. Come, the castle is not far away."

With a light step, Thea led the way through the forest. The sun had set, leaving a hush over the land. The man followed Thea, his gait somewhat halting and unsteady and his rags catching on the briars as he went. The old warden went behind rejoicing softly.

When they reached the castle, servants came running out with torches to light the way for the queen but halted in their steps when they saw the uncouth man at her side and the strange shining on the face of the warden. "Have no fear," said Thea, "all is well. Henceforth our country will have a king. See, this is he!"

Unable to disobey her who had hitherto been their sovereign, the people welcomed their new king, albeit the welcome was quiet and subdued for no one understood what had come to pass. But in the days to follow, seeing Thea serve the new king with a humbleness and joy they had never seen in her in the days of her own queenship, the people soon learned to follow her example and in so doing, they saw their new king begin to shine like the sun when the clouds are driven apart by a fresh wind. And whereas Thea's reign had been one of early morning coolness when the dew lies on the grass and the moon appears on the sky as transparent as the host, the present reign was like the day at noon when the sun sheds its golden light like wine upon the earth.

Yet ever and again, the king turned to Thea for counsel and the magic of her wisdom; indeed she was as dear to him as life itself.

ON A GREEN CLEARING

In a grey and sprawling city there lived a young man—we can call him Erwin. When he was a young child and his life still like a flower, he dreamed he was one of the chosen ones of the world, destined to lead others to happiness and light. He saw himself as a torch bearer, burning with courage and the love of goodness, going ahead of his fellow-men, calling them to march behind him on the road to ultimate redemption. Or he was the wise and beloved ruler of a state that led the world in the perfection of its institutions under his unerring guidance.

As Erwin grew into adulthood, his dreams shrank and a sense of shame took their place for his life turned out to be in no way outstanding and he knew only too well how little he was master of the web of circumstance that wove itself around him, let alone master of anyone else.

Erwin took up work in the office of a building firm when he became a man and he rarely remembered his childhood dreams, for he was bent on fitting himself into the patterns of ordinary life. Only occasionally—perhaps in rounding the corner of an empty street in the twilight, or in walking through the quiet park in the midst of the roar of the traffic in the city—did the dormant urges of his youth rise up in him in a sudden flash of powerful longing, causing him to feel for a moment as if the axis of the earth itself had trembled. Then the old sense of shame at his own smallness made him redden even in his solitude. Yet deep inside in a place where shame cannot enter, a voice cried out in him: O, why must life be like a prison? Why can I not live as I longed to live when I was a child? It was a sad cry like that of a bird flying over the bare furrows in the early spring, not sensing the hope and the promise they held.

After such moments Erwin would again struggle to maintain himself in the set pattern of his life, trying to suppress the cry of longing, for to listen to it made him feel either too large or too small for his place in ordinary existence.

One morning when Erwin arrived at the office, he was called to see the chief of the firm for which he worked. "Young man," said the chief at his desk, "I should like to give you a chance to improve your position in the firm and if you agree to undertake an immediate commission, your possibilities might better themselves from next week onwards."

Although Erwin flushed with pleasure and embarrassment, he felt an undercurrent of apprehension lest he become further committed to this firm, but he answered the chief: "Sir, if you think I can be of greater service to the firm, I shall be glad to carry out any instructions you may give me."

The chief smiled and said: "The task is this. You must travel tomorrow to R… You will have to take the bus that leaves early in the morning as there is no through train to R… You will arrive at half past four in the afternoon. Go straight to Mr. N. at the G… factory and lay before him the plan enclosed in this envelope I shall give you which you shall study carefully tonight. It is essential you come to terms of agreement not later than Sunday. Tomorrow is Friday; on Saturday the G… factory is closed so you do not have much time. Now tell me, will you take this on?"

"Yes, sir," said Erwin "I shall try my best."

"Very well," said the chief, "here is the envelope; everything depends on your understanding of its content and on the way you will convey its meaning."

Very early the next morning, Erwin rose to catch his bus. There were not many other passengers and he settled comfortably for the long journey ahead. He dozed fitfully while the bus rumbled through the empty streets of the city until it reached the open country. Then he sat up and looked out of the window. Although it was spring and the trees were in bud, a chilly north wind was blowing in gusts over the countryside and the sky was leaden and unfriendly. Erwin drew the envelope out of his pocket to go over its contents once again. He was still bewildered by the project his chief had drawn up. It seemed keen enough and Erwin saw that it would not only affect his own firm and the G… factory but many other concerns as well, yet its aims and purposes seemed obscure, something vital seemed to be lacking and he wondered what he would be able to say to Mr. N… to persuade him to accept the plan. He began to feel entirely insufficient for the task ahead and wished he had never taken it on.

Outside the chill wind carried hail and sleet in its rough gusts and desolation lay over the countryside—the desolation that comes when the promise of spring is revoked.

The bus went on through towns and hamlets, stopping here and there, but there was little to be seen for now it was snowing heavily—the hedges, the fields, the roofs of houses were white and the road too was covered. The few passengers began to discuss the phenomenon of snow in spring and Erwin as he listened felt an uneasy thought threading its way to his mind: Would the bus arrive on time? His chief had timed his meeting at the G… factory exactly. What would happen if something went wrong? Feverish worry took possession of Erwin and the remarks of his fellow passengers about the weather and its tricks did little to relieve his anxiety.

On the bus went through the whitened landscape, going slowly to keep to the slippery road. At last it began to ascend a long hill—it was four o'clock.

"R… is not far," said the conductress to Erwin, "it is only two miles from the top of the hill."

Then I shall easily make it, thought Erwin and a faint sense of excitement took the place of worry. Near the top of the hill the bus began to choke and jerk and then it stopped. The driver got out and after a few minutes he announced engine trouble. "There'll be another bus along here in half an hour's time," he said, "anyone who would like to wait for it can do so."

Erwin was the only one who got out of his seat: "I must be in R… in half an hour's time—I'll walk on." As he left the bus he did not notice that he had forgotten the envelope—it lay on the empty seat.

Erwin took to the road and after a few minutes the lights of the standing bus receded into the gathering twilight. Away ahead a few lights gleamed in the distance on the left. That must be R…, Erwin thought, I'll make it just in time. The snow was falling in thick flakes. Erwin pulled his coat collar up over his ears and trudged on, occasionally glancing up at the dark telephone poles which were his only guide as the road itself was now hidden under the snow. In his mind, he began rehearsing his meeting with Mr. N… but strain his thoughts as he might he could not get beyond the first words of greeting.

All at once he ran up against a stately iron gate. He looked around and saw no telegraph poles, no lights in the distance, nothing but the iron gate before him. By the light of a match he looked at his watch and saw that it was nearly half past four. Despair took possession of him; he felt like throwing himself down in the snow and sobbing like a little child that has been cheated. How could he have missed the way? Now all was lost—he had failed.

It seemed useless to turn back and as the iron gate gave to his touch, he pushed it open and followed a little path that led into the wood beyond. Everything was silent. Here and there stood groups of spotted deer, shadowy in the dying daylight. They did not stir as Erwin passed, but stared after him for a while and then went on pawing the snow-sprinkled ground for food. Erwin did not notice them for his eyes were filled with tears. The path dipped downward after a little into a wide clearing. Great forms rose up in the gloom ahead and for a moment he thought he had come upon a sleeping village, but drawing nearer, he perceived the massive ruins of an ancient abbey. They stood sombrely in their roofless dignity, and utter stillness was around them. Filled with misery and cold, Erwin sat down on the stump of a tree at the edge of the clearing and putting his head on his knees, he tried to achieve a state of oblivion in which nothing could hurt or touch him.

A slight sound made him look up. In front of him on the green grass the sun was shining into the clearing. The air was warm and sweet. A band of monks and craftsmen appeared, the latter carrying their tools, the former singing as they went. In the centre of the clearing they formed a wide circle on the dew-wet grass. A white haired monk stepped into the centre of the circle and began to speak of the glory of Christ in the daylight, in the growing of the corn, in the lilt of the song of the birds and in the shapes and moving of all living creatures as well as all the things of the earth that have no breathing life. Also in the souls of men Christ's glory shines—indeed it is there that it loves best to be, for Christ seeks the human heart above all else, because in its dim wine-warm chambers, the flame of love can best be kindled, and where men live and work and pray in brotherhood there

goes a shaft of living light from heart to heart, forming the beams of a temple that unite the parts and carry the weight of the great roof above. The weight of the world, its suffering and sorrow rest securely on the rafters of human love. "Let us, O my brothers, build a house of peace so that we and others may worship in it and contemplate the power of the Word that was in the beginning and that made all things, the Word of Love. Let us be industrious, knowing that each step we take, each raising of our hands in labour, each thought that flickers through the vault of our minds, if performed in the awareness of Him will hallow this ground and make it good. For who, then, are the priests of Christ if not those who build on earth, who work on earth, who love on earth? Let us set the mark of God upon this green place, O my brothers. May His Son be among us! Let the beams of our church be of light, the arches be of faith and let the stones be set so that they may sing in harmony, O brothers, of our great joy that Christ is with the earth!"

Erwin watched with wonder as the monks and the craftsmen began to trace out the plans of the abbey in the clearing. He perceived that the lengths and widths and heights were dictated by the high order of the stars that shone down in invisible light upon that place. He saw the men begin to hew the building stones from the nearby cliffs and to haul them to the centre of the clearing. So the building of the abbey began.

Erwin also saw what perhaps those monks and craftsmen did not see in the fervour of their work: he saw Christ over the green field, His Body like a light-filled Host, standing amidst the grey stones, shedding unseen living strength into the hearts of the toiling men, uniting their endeavours with the will of His Father. The abbey rose up, shining, a harmonious house of peace, a gleaming witness to human striving, a grey stone witness to the power of the Risen Christ.

Erwin rose to his feet. The clearing was dark and still. He took the path he had come by. It led him back through the wood to the iron gate and then onto the road. It had stopped snowing. The wind had died away leaving the air milder. In the near distance, the lights of a town twinkled. Erwin went along the road down the hill that led into the town which was R… according to its sign of welcome. He took a room at an inn and slept peacefully until the next morning.

It was a grey day but soft and windless. Thaw had set in and the snow was fast melting. Everywhere Erwin heard the sound of running, dripping water along the streets and under the bridges and from the eaves of the houses. Although he knew that the G… factory was closed for the day, he felt an urge to see it from the outside. It stood at the edge of the town in a large fenced-in enclosure—a long low cement building with windows and doors that seemed hollow and empty like the eyes of a blind man. The asphalt paths glinted dully under the mournful sky; the stillness that lay over the enclosure seemed void of that generating power that otherwise lies in the intervals between sounds. Yet a feeling of warmth welled up in Erwin for all that the factory represented—the many men whose hours of work animated that cement block during the week, the efforts, the forethought, the laying aside of personal desires to work for the whole. He saw how that whole was part of another greater Whole—the vast structure of mankind. Each grey cement factory in the world was like a tomb into which human hopes had sacrificed themselves. The stones of the abbey were also tombstones of human endeavour, but the abbey was built out of the power of resurrection and human labour was transformed into human love. The factories of the world must not remain dumb graves out of which false ghosts arise to haunt the millions of men in the world, sowing illusions and anxiety. Out of the tombstones of all industry, there must rise the sure knowledge that the earth and all it contains is hallowed by Christ and that everything men do is an acknowledgement of His Presence.

As Erwin walked up and down in front of the empty factory, many new thoughts crowded into his mind. He struggled for the grains of truth in the myriad floods of brightness that poured into his heart. As he walked back into the town, he was stirred by an uncertain certainty—he felt neither too small nor too large, but sensed a new strength rising up within him.

The next morning, Erwin woke to the sounds of church bells. It was bright and warm and the birds sang loudly; sunlight shone onto the town and the outlying fields. A bus was due to return to the city and Erwin went out in front of the inn to wait for it. When the bus came, Erwin boarded it and found one empty seat beside an elderly fine looking man to whom he immediately felt drawn in sympathy.

After a while, he and his companion began talking. The latter told Erwin that he was travelling to the city to contact the director of a large building firm in connection with a plan of construction he had sent him. “Strange,” said Erwin’s companion “it was sent to me by bus in an open envelope.” He pulled the envelope Erwin had left in the bus two days before out of his pocket. “I have read through the plan,” he said “it is keen enough, but in a sense futile. I cannot see its purpose; it seems incomplete. I wonder why they sent no one to explain.” “I think I can explain,” said Erwin and he began to go through the project point by point in the light of what he had seen and heard on the green clearing behind the iron gate. The plan assumed reality.

Erwin and his new friend and his chief became a little band of men, a tiny cell of light in a vast dim organism. They did not achieve great changes and outwardly they were as they had been before. Yet the three formed a building stone of inward light, waiting for other building stones of like substance to be set side by side with them to the end that one day human industry will build abbeys of selfless service on green clearings.

St. John's Tide

THE HAVEN

Once upon a time, though it was not long ago—it might have been yesterday, it could well have been tomorrow—a young man set out to wander. He had no aim ahead, he left no friends behind; he was like flotsam bobbing on an ocean, driven along when the winds blow, floating inertly when the winds drop.

And indeed the countryside through which he wandered was not unlike an ocean with its rising hills descending into valleys to rise again, and the soft summer breezes rippling over the corn and stirring the billowing treetops. Our young man drifted through the ever-changing colours and shapes of the countryside as little boats drift out at sea, passing hamlets and villages and crofts and lone houses—all like little harbours where ships can anchor safely, sheltered from the trails of the ocean. When the young man observed the farmers at work in their fields, he saw that the great earth held them to her breast, not letting them stray or wander, and he knew that he himself was afraid of the bonds of the earth or for that matter, of any bonds that labour might impose or fetters that the love of men might forge. He preferred to remain adrift and to keep to the fringes of places where men live and work and to observe all things from a distance.

Stillness lay over the land and the same stillness reigned up over the densely wooded hills. No leaf, no blade of grass stirred and Henry, as we will call him, heard not a sound but the crunching of his own shoes upon the pebbles on the way. High up over the rising hills ahead, storm clouds were churning up and flashes of dull orange lightning streaked across the darkening skies. Thunder rumbled as if from the roots of the hills. Down in the valley where Henry walked, the breathless air quivered in the heat of a summer's day. He walked on up towards the great oak forest ahead, sweat running down his body. The black turmoil of storm clouds was rolling over the crest of the hill down into the valley. There was a faint sulphuric smell. As Henry reached the edge of the forest, a wild whisper sighed over the corn fields and in through the forest, whipping up the treetops; the great oak branches swayed in circles—the storm broke.

Lightning danced in and over the forest where Henry sheltered, accompanied by the drums of thunder and swathed in sheaths of rain, and all the growing things seemed to applaud, until the storm passed on to other valleys and meadows far off, leaving the forest gently dripping and the corn glistening in the shy evening sunlight in the wake of the storm.

Although Henry was wet to the skin, he did not turn back to the valley in search of shelter for the night; indeed the last croft he had passed lay far back out of sight. Up through the trees, he caught sight of a low stone wall running along a gentle slope in the forest. He decided to follow the wall, thinking that it would doubtless lead him to human habitation.

Night fell as Henry felt his way along the wall, but it was a light night for it was high up in the north where the light of one day lingers to meet the light of the next. The grey stone wall wound its way steadily upwards through the oaks until it straightened out, leading Henry out into a wide clearing in the forest; the great trees stood round the clearing like pillars on guard. Above the forest shone the green-blue light of the northern sky.

In the midst of the clearing there stood a large house, its windows ablaze with lights from within and soft white mists hovering over the surrounding grounds. From the distance it looked like a huge ship sailing on a darkening sea. As he went towards the house through the wet grasses, Henry heard the lilt of music and the nearer he drew, the louder it became, now mingled with the sound of laughter. The portal of the house was wide open and a broad shaft of warm light flooded out onto the lawn and seemed to invite the wayfarer in.

Henry stepped into the light and found himself in the midst of a bright crowd of people who were dancing in a great hall lit by hundreds of little lights. It appeared to him that his entry had not gone unnoticed; he was straightaway swept in amongst the whirling figures of the dance, one partner in his arms at one moment, another the next. A tall, somewhat elderly handsome man, a knight, led the dance and called out the intricate patterns which Henry performed faultlessly although he had never danced before. Most of the ladies and the men were dressed in velvets and silks, although a few of them went about in rougher habit and seemed irked by the music and laughter. These latter wore nothing on their heads, but to Henry it seemed that the others wore tiny coronets.

At one end of the hall, Henry caught a glimpse of a golden chair like a throne as he whirled past in the dance, but it seemed that it was not reserved for any one person, although he would have been curious to see the master of the house. Anyone who desired could sit on the throne for a bit, but then had to relinquish it to another. Henry himself was at one moment almost flung onto the golden seat as he lost his balance in the press of the dance. He blushed deeply to think of himself sitting on a throne and hoped that no one witnessed his embarrassment. Nonetheless, he thought he observed that glances in his direction grew warmer and more friendly after this and a strange new feeling of exhilaration took possession of him and he laughed and danced with deep joy.

At the height of the dance, a quickening drink was served. Henry gazed into the glowing liquid before he put it to his lips; he saw his own reflection in a new light. All eyes watched him and their friendly look was as heartening as the drink which he drank to the last drop.

Dawn began to lighten the clearing outside and the surrounding trees and fields became visible through the windows. Inside the house, the little lights began to flicker and fade. A deep bell rang from somewhere and one by one the dancers slipped away, leaving the hall empty and still. Henry was the last to go. He found himself in a little room containing a couch. Overwhelmed by something more than just tiredness, he lay down and slept.

He woke to the sound of children's voices. Outside on the lawn many children of all ages were gathered with their teachers. Some were playing games. A few quiet children sat to one side busy at some handicraft; a group of little ones were making daisy chains. Beyond the low stone wall by which Henry had come to this place he saw older children at work in the vegetable garden and further on, others tending flowers and herbs. Out on the fields, boys and girls were helping the men and from everywhere came the sound of work being done and of the joy in doing it.

Henry went out onto the lawn and the children crowded around him, wishing him a good day; their teachers stood by watching and smiling. Everywhere in the eyes of children and teachers alike, although not in all, Henry recognised the dancers of the night before. How different they looked on this bright morning!

The gardener, hearing the shouts of the children on the lawn around Henry, leaned over the wall to add his greeting to theirs. Henry went to him, followed by the children. The gardener was a tall man, somewhat older, dressed in a blue overall stained with earth; his hands were strong and rough from work. When Henry looked into his face, he saw the deep warm look in the eyes of the tall knight who led the dance during the night that had just passed. A smile played around the gardener's lips when he perceived Henry's recognition.

Henry's senses swam in the light of the gardener's smile; in the depths of his being, he heard a strange, infinitesimal sound—like the rattle of the chain that slips through the bottom of the ship to let its anchor down.

THE QUEEN OF THE VALLEY

When he was a student, Iain spent his summers wandering with his rucksack on his back. In the course of the summers of his youth, he had walked through many a country, seen many a beautiful thing and exchanged words with many a stranger in passing by.

Iain grew older and became a teacher rather than a student and he no longer wandered alone. He spent his years wrapped in the life of his family; the wanderings of his youth gave way to the stiller reflections of later years.

One mild evening, Iain sat at his desk weary from the day's work. Looking out of the window into the green of the trees in the park, he let his mind wander whithersoever it wished, just as a rider sometimes slackens the reins and lets his horse choose the way…

He went along a winding dusty road that led from the broad country beyond into a narrow little valley. He had often walked along that road and knew its every bend; even the herbs growing on either side seemed to greet him as an old friend. It was a pretty valley, one of the countless in that deeply furrowed land. On the slopes of its hills lay fields and woods and up on the ridges grew tall trees, standing guard over the valley below. Somewhere where the road took a bend there was a quiet little village with hardly so much as a square to boast of; a few old houses in tired colours and a little stone church higher up, away from the road. Barely had a traveller entered the village, he was out again at the other end. Yet it was here, in and around the little village that Iain had encountered a strange power that compelled him to walk that way time and again.

A little river flowed through the valley, winding and twisting as much as the road although not always in concordance with it. Sometimes it flowed close to the road with a gesture of friendliness, and sometimes it bounded off over stones and disappeared as if to show its independence. The little river was lined on either side by birch trees and willows in part, then by moist pastures, then again by rough rocks with dark fir trees growing here and there between. The valley was narrow and often full of shadows and coolness where the many greens of the trees merged in the evening mists and the silvery streaks of the running water glinted in the gathering dimness.

It was at sunset that Iain first came down into the valley. The evening shadows had risen up the steep slopes towards the trees on the ridges and the valley lay wrapped in cool blueness. But above the ridges everything was still shining in the light of the evening sun. The full soft summer clouds towered upwards imbued with the grace and majesty of the glow of the setting sun, their rolling folds filled with a deep rosy hue like the folds of a flowing garment. And far above the rosy forms of the clouds and the still blue of the valley beneath, shone the bright transparency of heaven, almost revealing the golden world of the angels. Beholding this majestic picture, Iain had the feeling of a queenly presence. Then the clouds drifted away, shifting and changing and dissolving. The transparency above deepened into indigo and the stars shone through from the bright world beyond.

Although Iain never saw just that image again, he did not lose the feeling of a queenly presence in and over the valley. Once as he was walking through the birch wood after a summer thunder storm, breathing in the sweet freshness of the teeming grasses while the soft green leaves of the trees still glistened with wetness, Iain looked up over the fields and saw a rainbow spanning the clearing skies, its one end dipping down into the steaming meadows in the valley, its other end disappearing behind the hills into other valleys beyond. Lost in the contemplation of the ethereal embrace of the rainbow and the upward surrender of the earth to its radiance, Iain felt her presence again; brightly clothed and imbued with the hues of heaven, yet fashioned out of the warmth and the matter of the earth, out of the goodness and the motherliness of the soil. And then she was gone and with her the shining colours of the rainbow and the infinite serenity of the moment.

And often in the shimmering heat lying over the meadows and the cornfields or along the cool edges of the forests high up on the ridges of the hills or around the bend of the road where the ox-carts still rumble into the village in the evening—or in the soft dim shadows of the byres where the cows stand side by side, sighing and munching—Iain seemed to catch glimpses of the hem of her garment or a tress of her rippling wheat-gold hair as she passed by like the breath of a wind, leaving behind her a wine-red glow held in bonds of blue, never to be summoned at will, yet all-pervading in and over that quiet little valley.

In his mind, Iain called her his 'Queen of the Valley,' and smiled when he thought how little the simple little village knew of its sovereign 'Queen'—for Iain never spoke of his visions to any person there or elsewhere…

Thus his mind wandered into the past, and now the past seemed to surge towards him like a great wave engulfing him, and out of that submergence was born the decision to once again visit that far away little valley.

Iain again left the open country and took the road leading into the valley. In the distance he saw the hills he knew so well and at the wayside grew the familiar herbs. Years lay between that moment and the last time he had looked down onto the village at the bend in the road. As he drew near the village, the years seemed to fall away, leaving nothing but a tiny residue in the depths of his being that was more of the nature of the quality than the quantity of time.

All at once, Iain realised that however often he had been in the village before, he had never been inside its little church. Looking up at its modest stone tower, he felt a strong urge to enter it and quickened his steps. On either side of the road there were the familiar sights that once caused him to linger in the pleasure of seeing them again, but now he regarded them with a faint sense of impatience and passed them by hurriedly for fear they might hold him back.

A little path wound steeply upwards behind the houses to the church. Iain entered and looked around. It was cool and clean and no different from many another village church. He felt a sharp sense of disappointment—why had he so wanted to come here?

Someone hitherto unnoticed opened a door into a chapel at the side of the church. Iain turned and looked through the open door. Over the altar hung a picture of the Virgin and Child. She sat in a robe of glowing red with a stream of blue flowing around her shoulders. Her hair the colour of golden wheat rippled down her back. She sat beneath the tender luminescent arch of the rainbow and above her was the bright transparency of the heavenly sky. Shining with ethereal colour, yet fashioned out of the warmth of the motherhood of the earth and truly queenly, she held her Child on her knee.

Iain stayed long in the cool little chapel before the painting of the master, pondering on the mysterious union between Nature and Art.

A SUMMER DREAM

A summer day dawned. But could one call the sultry increase of grey light that crept over the dull roofs and dusty streets of the city, dawn? The city seemed to emerge out of the oven of the night and now lay steaming under a molten sky. The leaves of the city trees looked metallic, like little spades that prod the heaviness hanging over them. The life of the city began with a whirr of traffic, a whirr that grows louder and louder until it reaches the roaring pitch at which it remains throughout the day, to sink suddenly into an uncertain lull at some imperceptible moment of the night.

Ivan awoke with an aching head and heavy limbs. The dull thought that his office was closed for the day did not stir any enthusiasm in him, instead—the old question of which he lived in constant creeping dread loomed up before him: What is the use of it all? Although Ivan feared that question, he was accustomed to its presence. He encountered it every morning when he awoke; it accompanied him to his work and it waited for him in the evening. He seldom lost its companionship. And so this morning, he arose and trying not to give in to his insidious companion, he resolved to spend the day at the seaside.

In due course, Ivan arrived at the station and took his place in a long queue, shuffling slowly towards the ticket office. In spite of the heat, he lost his companion for a bit and his mind was occupied with the thought of his destination. On the platform, he joined another queue that was sluggishly making its way through the barrier like a disjointed snake. Waves of hot choking steam gushed out from underneath the locomotives and Ivan's companion returned to him with full force: What is the use of it all? What is the use of it all? It was not through his own will that he boarded the crowded train for his companion had paralysed his will, but there is something that determines much of what we do, that shepherds us here and there whatever our companions may be. It is called 'convention' and it helps to obey it at moments when one is bereft of one's own determination.

Ivan found a seat in a compartment and as he greeted his fellow passengers, his companion seemed to retire. A faint sense of expectancy stirred in his breast and became so persistent that it drove him to stand at the window in the corridor. The station sheds, the platforms and warehouses were passing by with increasing speed; a gentle breeze blew in at the window, a breeze that became fresher, lighter, cleaner the further away from the city the train travelled.

At last the train arrived at Ivan's destination. He joined the line of luggage-carrying, pushing people in the corridor. As he stepped down off the train with another passenger at his heels, the familiar voice whispered at the back of his mind, but again as he crossed the platform to reach the exit, he felt the breath of salt air coming from beyond the dunes and recovered his sense of expectancy.

He now threaded his way down through the main street of the village towards the beach. It was crowded with people wandering in and out of the shops. A smell of petrol and dust filled Ivan's nostrils and with dismay, he knew his companion was close. Struggling to fight him off, Ivan strained his eyes to catch a glimpse of the sea ahead; there it lay, blue and shining beneath the clear, clean sky beyond the village. He quickened his steps and soon reached the well-kept public gardens between the houses and the beach. Gulls circled screaming overhead; Ivan heard the sound of breaking waves and all at once, he was on the beach.

A dense crowd of people was spread out over the stretch of sand; cabins, deck chairs, umbrellas in bright colours broke the line of the sunburnt multitude, knit together in a bond of conformity. That sense of loneliness which can overcome a man standing at the edge of a large crowd overcame Ivan; it is the loneliness that does not realise that the conformity it cannot enter is by far the greater loneliness. Ivan did not know that the companion that haunted his own life haunts the lives of most men. He did not perceive him going amongst the crowd from one person to another—did not see the sudden halting of a smile on the face of a running girl, the hidden look of deep shy anxiety in the eyes of those who shouted and laughed loudest—as the dark one went his pitiless way through the hearts and minds of the multitude—What is the use of it all?

Ivan turned away from the beach and wandered back through the village until he came to the open country beyond. Meadows lay on either side of the road. Red poppies and blue chicory grew in amongst the young corn and the sweet smell of freshly cut hay filled the air. Away from the salt tang of the sea breeze and the ceaseless sound of the waves, Ivan felt the soft protection of the fertile earth and thought of his mother who had long since died. The crowds on the beach and his sense of loneliness faded and gave way to a feeling of gentle emptiness. Ahead lay a range of low wooded hills. The heat of the sun was intense and haze quivered on the road and over the fields. Ivan began to long for the shade and went steadily along the hot dusty road towards the hills.

At last he reached the woods and a wave of relief flooded through him as he stepped into the cool shade of the trees. It was like entering a dimly lit cathedral, he thought, for the branches of the trees formed high arches overhead and their great grey trunks were like pillars. Ivan had never experienced the sanctity of a forest before and he was overawed by its stillness. Not a sound did he hear as he stepped over the carpet of moss mingled with pine needles on the floor of the forest.

No bird sang, no creature hopped about, no breeze stirred. The deeper into the forest he went, the more it seemed like a cathedral. The sun shone through the mottled green leaves as though through stained glass windows and Ivan almost expected to come across something like an offering table or an altar. Suddenly a small clearing opened up before him in the midst of which there grew wild roses in full bloom, breathing out a tender spicy fragrance. A hawk hovered overhead and above the treetops he caught glimpses of the white chalk crowns of distant hills gleaming in the sunlight. Ivan was hungry but had brought nothing to eat with him. He lay down in the shade of the thicket of wild roses on the soft grass; bees hummed in the blossoms—high above the hawk seemed to hover in eternity. He no longer felt lonely; he was livingly alone in the presence of an unknown force.

He was suddenly startled by a sound and jumped to his feet. Beyond the wild roses, he caught sight of the opening of a cave in the rocks. A man emerged from within—very old but as tall and slender as a youth, or was he a youth? In his hands he carried a jug of water and a loaf of bread. Ivan felt his hunger like a wave of pain and groaned faintly. In that moment two ravens flew up out of the cave and vanished into the trees; the man looked up and saw Ivan and perceived his hunger.

"Come," he said, "you need sustenance. Share this bread with me."

Drawn by some gentle magic, Ivan approached the cave and sat down on the ground at the man's behest and took the bread and the water he was given. He felt refreshed and strengthened as he had never felt before.

The sun had begun to wester and Ivan thanked the man and rose to go. The man himself seemed to grow transparent and recede into the inner recesses of the cave. Suddenly Ivan cried out: "Tell me before you go who you are; I almost know it, but not quite."

The man's eyes shone with an indescribably tender light: "I am the one who is waiting till He comes."

"And will He come?" cried Ivan, the tears running down his face.

"Yes. He will come softly in the darkness of men's doubts, their anguish, their loneliness; only wait and listen to His footsteps in the depths of your longing heart."

Ivan awoke.

A MODERN FAIRY TALE

In the midst of a city of today lived a man whose name could have been Diogenes because, like the cynic of old, he lived in a barrel. It was a barrel of his own making, it stood at the foot of a bridge and was bound about by three iron bands, and from the dimness inside it, Diogenes could look down the busy thoroughfare that opened into the central square of the city.

On the left side of the square stood the grey stone universities, the inside halls of which Diogenes knew well for he had sought the truth of knowledge there and had listened to lectures on philosophy, natural philosophy, moral philosophy, and had worn for a while the white coat of the scientist in the research laboratories. But he had left the austere enclosures of the universities with a residue of dead thoughts in his mind which slowly hardened into the one iron band around his barrel.

Across the square to the right, rose the steeples, cupolas and gilded crosses of the many churches which Diogenes also knew well. In them he had learned that the Decalogue is the final criterion of man's moral life, or he had been obliged to accept this or that dogma. To the back of the churches were the many obscure and winding streets in which were the meeting-places of sects and occult organisations through which Diogenes had continued his search for the meaning of life. From this search he had emerged with a chainwork of temporal concepts which became the second band around his barrel.

At the head of the square, the flags of many nations fluttered over the roofs of the buildings dedicated to the betterment of social conditions, to political enlightenment in the East-West question, to the progressive handling of the racial problem, and to world trade. For a time, Diogenes had worked at the countless desks of this world-building until the illusions engendered in its air-conditioned offices drove him into complete isolation from his fellow-men. This isolation was the third band around Diogenes' barrel.

Not wanting to confess that his life was being crushed by the iron bands around his soul and mind, Diogenes turned his back on the strongholds in the centre of the city and wandered aimlessly up and down the main streets, taking jobs in newspaper offices, insurance offices, advertising firms, department stores and the like. Finally, he tried public transport in an effort to get somewhere himself, but gradually he ceased striving, ceased being touched by any thing or person, ceased trying to understand. He was not even a cynic like the Diogenes of old; the core of his existence merged with the three iron bands that strangled his soul—the iron bands of social isolation, religious unbelief, and self-destructive thought.

One day a shaft of light fell across the dimness that had gathered around the opening of Diogenes' barrel. He, peering through the accustomed gloom, saw a stranger, a woman, gazing thoughtfully at his barrel. A deep, forgotten feeling of unease stirred his soul and increased when he saw that in her hand she carried the staff of Mercury. A physician was the last thing he wanted; to accept help would only mean stirring up the old chaos. He looked up into the woman's face. In that moment, she spoke in a clear voice: "Can I do anything for you?" "Yes," said Diogenes, trembling, "you can move out of my darkness."

Just then she turned and saluted a man who was coming across the bridge; he was her teacher and master, and she joined a group of pupils who went to meet him on the bridge. The air over the bridge seemed especially clear and alive, so much so that the darkness in Diogenes' barrel lessened.

The master began to speak to his pupils and friends on the bridge and Diogenes could not help but hear his words. Looking over to the grey stone buildings of the universities, the master spoke of the necessity of science to arrive at a recognition of the spirit that moves behind all matter and of the spiritual origin of the earth. Turning towards the churches, he spoke of the necessary freedom of thought that will have to enter the sphere of religion if the living facts of Christianity are not to be overlooked. And lastly pointing to the buildings dedicated to the social problems of the world, the master spoke of the need for the right understanding of the nature of man—the Anthropo-Sophia—which alone is the antidote for the isolation into which the individual of today is more and more enclosed.

When he finished speaking, he went on into the city, followed by his pupils and friends. Evening cast a golden light over the roofs and cupolas around the square; Diogenes crept out of his barrel and straightened up. He looked over to the city into which the master had gone. Rosy clouds hovered above the golden roofs and gleaming windows; a long-forgotten fairy tale rose from the depths of his soul and seemed to enact itself again in the clouds above the city: the fairy tale of the king's daughter who once had a golden ball which she played with in the castle garden, throwing it higher and higher until one day it fell into a deep well and was lost. The princess mourned for her golden ball until out of the bottom of the well came an ugly frog who promised to retrieve the golden ball if she would marry him. The princess promised and the frog brought back the golden ball, but the princess did not keep her promise to the ugly frog and refused to unite with him, incurring the wrath of her father, the king. But the frog persisted and stayed near her and in the end, in an act of desperation, she flung the ugly creature against the wall and he was transformed into a prince, and the wedding was celebrated with great joy.

Up from the gleaming domes of the churches of the city rose the image of the princess; her golden ball hovered over the roofs of the university buildings, and from the cellars of the social centre at the head of the square emerged the ugly frog, and the three—the golden ball of Spiritual Knowledge, the princess of living Religion and the ugly frog of human Social Misery who is in reality a prince became united.

All at once Diogenes heard a loud noise; the iron bands around the barrel of his existence snapped one by one, making him free and again able to live—and he realised that he himself was an element in that same fairy tale: Faithful Henry, not the Diogenes of antique times, but the servant the iron bands around whose heart burst asunder for joy that the princess of the golden ball was united with the Frog Prince.

Having now learned from the master on the bridge what it means to be a faithful servant of the conditions of his own times and not their victim, he crossed over the bridge and went into the city to look for the master in order to learn further from him of the forgotten meaning of life.

The Moral Background of Fairy Tales

A talk given at the annual conference of the Guild of Teachers of Backward Children in Bangor, Wales on 13th April 1961.

It is an age-old urge of the human mind to clothe truths in the garment of the parable or of the myth. Take, for instance, the myths of ancient Persia, Egypt, Greece: here we have the great geological events of the evolution of the earth, the early wanderings of peoples at the dawn of history, the founding of cultures, and the development of conscious thinking—clothed in images full of colour, depth and drama which impart infinitely more of the quality of human becoming than do any of the scientific theories of evolution. All myths spring from realities however 'mythological' their imagery may be. Take the opening chapter of Genesis—if I may speak of it in this context: condensed into a few verses, we have the drama of the relationship of man to his Creator and to creation, and where else can we encounter so profoundly the most fundamental of human problems—the Fall of Man from divine grace—as in the grand economy of the pictures in the opening chapter of Genesis?

Then we have the sagas: the Iliad, the Odyssey, the Mahabharata, the Edda and many others. These sagas relate the biographies of heroes, dynasties and clans with whom were identified the rise and fall of cultures, races and peoples. The sagas, interwoven as they are with the wonderful, are born out of the soil of actual events, are vast tapestries whose threads are as real as any strand of linen or silk.

Later come the legends of Christian times. Legends are based less upon external actualities, but are rather accounts of human attributes and virtues in conflict with all that is temporal in the human constitution. But because the legend deals with the miracles of human ethics, it cannot be said to be fictitious, to be untrue.

It would appear that truth as it was, is and will be striven for by the human mind is frequently condemned to sterility unless a peculiar power comes to its aid: the power of imagery, the power of the parable which clothes the naked truth, allowing it to walk among the less philosophical, allowing it to take its place, so to speak, at the table of the lowliest. Consider the parables of the great gospel of parables—the Gospel of St. Matthew, and their opening formula: the Kingdom of Heaven is like unto

a man who made a marriage for his son—
a grain of mustard seed—
leaven which a woman took and hid in a measure of wheat—
a net—
a treasure hid in a field—
ten virgins which took their lamps—

Here the Master of human morality sets forth the profoundest truths of human existence in a wealth of imagery, imagery of the purest simplicity. There are times when the appearance of the naked truth in the chamber of the mind brings with it a chilling draft of nothingness. Truth, clothed in the myth, in the parable or in the prophetic garments of the Apocalypse, goes amongst men as a bringer of life, of health. And how many of the great teachers and masters of ancient and more modern times make use of the power of the parable to put forward the fruits of the search for the truth!

The parable, the myth, the saga and other forms are the garment of the truth, are the mantle that relieves the harshness, the starkness of truth. Yet the garment in its true sense is not a cover, it does not hide. Think of the flower of Greek sculpture: the flowing garment does not hide the truth of the form beneath—it enhances, it brings out the essential nature of the form, the body. All true imagery brings out the essential nature of a thing. And how tempted we are to make daily use of the metaphor, the simile, to express more potently to our fellow-men what we feel to be the essence of a situation. Every figure of speech however commonplace, for instance, 'It's like looking for a needle in a haystack' or 'He smokes like a chimney', springs from the same urge that brings to life the loftiest of parables, the urge to go to the heart of a matter.

What is this power that gives imagery to ideas? It is the power of fantasy. What do we know about the power of fantasy? The power of fantasy is of opposite nature to the power of intellect; intellect is the scientist in us, fantasy is the poet, the artist, in us. Fantasy springs from an entirely different source in the human make-up. (See *The Study of Man* by Rudolf Steiner.) The light which Rudolf Steiner throws upon this peculiar quality removes it from the dubious reputation it has earned by being misunderstood. How often do we say of a person: 'His ideas are fantastic' meaning that he is a person remote from realities, given to flights of fancy and wholly irresponsible. Yet true fantasy is not fantastic, is not something arbitrary and the product of whim. True fantasy is a sister-power to poesy, it is an ever-willing servant to the truth, it is the weaver of the parable and is at work as a life-bringing element in every individual to a greater or lesser degree. True fantasy is the moral fantasy of which the German poet, Novalis, spoke. It springs from the artistic freedom of the searching mind which at the same time recognises the laws that govern truth. The greater, the keener the search of the intellect, the freer, the more vivid the metaphor, the parable.

The power of fantasy is to be seen in its purest form in early childhood when the pursuits of the intellect have not yet taken possession of the individual and the world is experienced as being magical and wonderful. The power of fantasy drinks from the well of childhood and is itself the child in man.

The fable and the fairy tale are two special 'children' of fantasy and are thus nearest to the child. But like all other forms of fantasy, they too are governed by the laws of truth.

Fables depict the social-moral interplay of the good and evil characteristics and motives of human nature. In the search for the appropriate images for the various attributes of the human psyche, animal-forms are taken to set forth the innate essence of characteristics such as greed, avarice, jealousy, cowardice and the like. And as such, the fable, especially Æsop's fables, is of immense moral value to the child at a certain age when sermonising on right behaviour falls on deaf ears.

But we actually want to speak about the fairy tale. Fairy tales constitute a world in themselves about which very much could be said. The fairy tales of different lands can give us deep insight into the nature of the different peoples and their missions in the great community of mankind. It would be tempting to go into all this, but I have chosen the so-called Grimm's fairy tale as an example of what I would like to put forward because it is the most representative of the European fairy tale as well as the most 'humanised'. By the latter, I mean that it deals less with trolls, goblins and spirits of Nature, and more with the phenomena of the human psyche or let us say soul.

We should be clear concerning the origin of the Grimm's fairy tales. They were not 'written' by the brothers Grimm; they are not inventions, there is nothing arbitrary in them. They are treasures of wisdom handed down through generations by word of mouth, from grandmother to child and so on. And the brothers Grimm spent many years of their lives going about Germany, finding out the purest sources of the fairy tales, and we hear of how the one brother sat at the feet of a simple old woman, listening and listening and taking down her tales in the inimitable language of the wise of heart, to then present them in book-form to countless people. The brothers Grimm were mediators, not inventors.

At this juncture, I should like to mention the interesting and wonderful fact that in this our so very scientific age, more and more anthologies of fairy tales of the peoples of the world are published; even the United Nations has published an anthology of fairy tales of all countries as a contribution, so it says in the preface, towards uniting men.

I should now like to outline some of the main characteristics of these Grimm's fairy tales, assuming that we are all familiar with them. In observing the nature of these characteristics, we shall be able to arrive at an appreciation of the theme of our study.

An outstanding characteristic of the fairy tale is the strong element of improbability and impossibility. The important events that turn the tide occur at impossible moments and through improbable factors. How often is the impossible asked of the central figure, everything remaining fateful until the impossible has been achieved? Take the miller's daughter of whom it is said that she can spin straw into gold when we all—and especially the child—knows that she cannot spin straw into gold. And yet, the fairy tale can only draw to its right conclusion when the impossible is performed—when straw is spun into gold. This is a miracle the human mind can sometimes perform when it spins the chaff of empty thoughts into the gold of wisdom.

Then there is the fact that the laws of logic are alien to the fairy tale; there is a conspicuous lack of logic. There is also a complete disregard of perspective, time or distance. A giant is huge whether he is close by or far away over the ocean. Whether the princess sleeps for a hundred years or a day plays little part. Distances can be covered in minutes; things can be seen over vast stretches of space. It would appear that in a fairy tale it is the quality of things which counts, the very innate nature of things, not the quantity, the measurability of things.

Fairy tales are absolute; there is no compromise. The good is good, the evil, evil. There are no complexities; good and evil are like white and black. In the fairy tale, the evil is self-destructive, it does not lie in the nature of evil to persist. Think of the wicked stepmother who is asked: What would you do with a person who did such and such a thing? And the stepmother answers: I would condemn her to be put in a spiked barrel and rolled down the hill into the lake. The king then says: You have spoken. She has condemned herself. The absolute distinction between good and evil in the fairy tale is of like nature to the absolutism of the child at a certain age. Only when the child begins to emerge out of the magical world of childhood does the distinction between good and evil become more relative and therefore, complicated. It is like the merging and mingling of cardinal colours into hitherto unknown and complex hues. But do we not understand the many intermediate colours better if we know what the truly cardinal, original colours are? The child who has been allowed to experience good and evil as absolute elements can later on face the intricacies of human morality with much greater clarity than the child who has been thrust into the relativity of good and evil at too early an age.

Connected with the absolutism of the fairy tale is the seeming element of cruelty, but this is only an interpretation of the adult. Cruelty does occur in the 'invented' fairy tale, in the more morbid fairy tale such as Andersen's. In the Central European fairy tale, the so-called Grimm's, it is the knowledge that evil must needs destroy itself. The overcoming of evil is the ultimate consummation of every fairy tale in which evil occurs; never is the evil allowed to be victorious.

Another important feature of the fairy tale is the going forth: the going forth into the world, into the forest, the having to wander, to return home in transformed circumstances. Take Hansel and Gretel.

They are sent out into the forest by their wicked stepmother, they encounter evil in the form of the witch and having overcome it, they return over the wide blue lake on the back of the white duck to their father's house, to find that the wicked stepmother is no more. The fairy tale returns whence it came; it goes back to the fountain-head, to the origin, however hard the way might have been, however fraught with difficulties. Think of the measure of security, of faith this very element gives to the child, for does not every human life begin with being "sent out into the forest?" The trial, the ordeal is the core of many a fairy tale, also being enchanted, being put-under-a-spell. How profoundly expressive of the trials of every human life in conflict with its environment! And how often do we see the enchanted prince or the princess kept in the tower waiting for release in so many of our handicapped children?

The wedding is usually the culmination of the fairy tale. Think of Cinderella, of Many Furs, of Snow White, the miller's daughter and countless others. The union, the mystical marriage with the highest, the best, with that which we can only call the spiritual, the divine, in the human being is the goal, the fulfilment of the fairy tale.

Time does not allow me to speak of the many figures in the fairy tale—of the giants, the dwarfs, the stepmothers, of the tailor, the bear—and yet in them we may see expressed many of the deviations, the limitations in human development which relate the fairy tale in so intimate a way with our work for the handicapped child. But just because of this, I should like to mention one figure especially: that of the simpleton, the youngest son, the one who is lazy, more stupid than his elder brothers; the incapable one. How often is it just he who withstands the trial; to whom unexpected help comes and who wins the princess in the end! The fairy tale is not an admirer of the intellect; it is a lover of the inexperienced, of the powers of original innocence, it sees in simplicity the element upon which the course of events depends, whereas sophistication falls short.

I should finally like to mention the number three which governs the fairy tale. There are three sons, three little men in the wood, things are done three times over, and so on. It is interesting to observe that in the fairy tales of other countries, the number three does not appear to govern with the same invariability as it does in the Central European fairy tale. In the wholly delightful and colourful Russian fairy tale for instance there is a certain chaos and things can happen any number of times. But in the number three there is harmony; three is the Trinity, in it is entailed past, present and future, and we can trace a pattern of infinitesimal trinities right down into our every moment of daily life.

Let us imagine, for instance, that we go into a room. At first we take in what we find there—the furniture, the pictures on the wall, and also the people standing about in the room. This is the given scene which is presented to us upon entering the room. Now let us assume that there is someone in the room with whom we have had a difficult encounter. Seeing him there immediately causes an emotional reaction, often a painful one. The emotional reaction will now be followed by a decision as to what we are going to do next. We are either going to leave the room and avoid this person, or we are going to face him and try to improve the relationship between us. The fact that the room is as it is, is a given one, the emotional reaction that arose upon seeing the person in question was partly determined by factors external to us, but the action we are now going to take is purely our own and depends only upon our own moral decision. Here it is that we fail daily a hundred times. We fail to determine our actions by the right moral decision; we fall short of the rounding-off of these infinitesimal trinities of human relationships. But the fairy tale leads through to the end; only then is true freedom achieved.

I once had a little eight year old girl in my class. She was psychologically deeply disturbed and very backward in school. Her behaviour was largely determined by the lower drives of human nature on the one hand. On the other hand, she was a tight bundle of anxiety and not able to establish any genuine relationship to other people, not even to her parents. One day, I began to tell the fairy tale of the fisherman who catches the golden fish in his net. The fish begs to be spared and promises the fisherman the fulfilment of any wish as long as he does not tell his wife. The fisherman asks for a beautiful house and fine clothes for his wife. They are granted, but at night the wife gets the better of her husband, discovers his secret and drives him to ask for more. This betrayal happens three times over. When I came to this part of the story, I noticed that the little girl was suffering anguish. She put her hands up to her face and cried out: Stop! Stop! Don't say it!

I went on very quietly through the three betrayals and their consequences, leading the story to its end. In the little girl, a dam of anxiety and insecurity seemed to burst, allowing the flood to flow freely towards its release, and I can truly say that this fairy tale was the beginning of her way upwards, was the key to open the door behind which she was imprisoned. She began to learn in school and what is more, to establish good and strong contact to those around her.

In many of the fairy tales, the conditions we observe in our handicapped children can be seen beautifully drawn. Think of the Frog Prince. There is the princess playing with her golden ball—she is in an ideal state of self-concentration, we may even say that she is completely withdrawn. She is the autistic child which plays with the leaf, the bit of string, happy in its own world of isolation from any human contact. But the 'catastrophe' comes when the princess loses her ball and now has to depend on the ugly frog to retrieve it. Think of her difficulties of contact with that frog! Are not our autistic children princes and princesses and is not all human contact as distasteful to them as the frog is to the princess in the fairy tale? Yet in the end, contact is established. It is established drastically—by the princess herself flinging the frog against the wall, but it is definitely established and the frog turns out to be a prince and the wedding, which is the epitome of contact, is celebrated.

One of the inherent forces in the young child's life is fear, fear of the unknown. How often does even the well-protected child know that the wolf is under the bed at night? It would seem that the wolf is an archetypal image of fear in the young child, because how does it know that it is a wolf when it has never seen one in so-called reality? I once knew a little boy who suffered badly from anxiety at night. When asked what fairy tale he wanted to hear before going to sleep, he invariably asked for the story of the *The Wolf and the Seven Little Kids.* In this tale, the wolf represents the evil in that he pretends to be what he is not; he is falsehood personified and for the young child, there are few things more terrible than to experience falsehood in the adult world around him. This wolf devours six of the kids while mother goat is out. The seventh, the youngest, escapes and in the end when the wolf is asleep, mother goat cuts open his belly, frees her kids and sews stones into the wolf instead so that later when he goes to the well to drink, the weight of the stones causes him to fall into the water and drown. Falsehood destroys itself, and the life of the little family goes on joyously. The little boy knew the right medicine for his night-time fears.

The fairy tale is indeed health-bestowing, it is medicine for the tender soul that is fraught with the fear of growing up into an alien world of intricacies, and many a grown-up person will confess that he takes refuge in the fairy tale in times of stress!

In conclusion, I should like to gather up the threads I set forth when I outlined the characteristics of the fairy tale: the elements of the impossible, the lack of logic, the trial, the catharsis, the ultimate freedom, the marriage. Just these elements constitute a 'high' school for the cultivation of moral powers. What takes us through the dangers, the trials of life, the impossible situations, if not such powers such as courage, enthusiasm, sacrifice, love? Powers which are not governed by the laws of logic, which are not based on the laws of probability? What can be less logical than generosity or self-sacrifice? Yet just these are powers that lead forward in moments when the intellect fails. Courage, enthusiasm, compassion and love are true forces which come to our aid when the light of reason flickers and leaves us in darkness.

The person who has heard fairy tales told in childhood, who has sat at the feet of one who can tell them in the way they are intended is a person who goes through life with a companion. This 'companion' is his faith in the 'magic' powers of the soul that bestow life and blessing upon the sober reasonable world in which we live our daily lives. Such a person, having drunk at the fountain of the fairy tale, has tasted truly the 'water of life' in the most Christian sense.

The cultivation of moral powers is essential to the education of all children. In our handicapped children in whom the powers of the intellect have broken down, the moral powers often shine forth with the greater dignity and purity. We know that we must do everything we can to allow this dignity to become a strong staff upon which these children may lean on their later way through life. The fairy tale and all that it stands for morally is the birthright of every child.